Studies for a
BYRON
BIBLIOGRAPHY

Studies for a
BYRON
BIBLIOGRAPHY

by

Francis Lewis Randolph

SUTTER HOUSE
1979

Library of Congress Cataloging in Publication Data

Randolph, Francis Lewis, 1951-1974.
  Studies for a Byron bibliography.

    1. Byron, George Gordon Noël Byron, Baron, 1788-1824
—Bibliography. I. Title.
Z8139.R35 (PR4381)   016.821'7   79-13752
ISBN 0-915010-26-7

Publisher and distributor: ↙
  SUTTER HOUSE
  P.O. Box 212
  Lititz, Pa. 17543

PRINTED IN THE UNITED STATES OF AMERICA

CONTENTS

PART I
THE FIRST AND LATER EDITIONS
OF BRYON'S WORK

SECTION 1 — THROUGH 1815

SECTION 2 — 1816-1930

PART II

WORKS EDITED BY OTHER WRITERS IN WHICH BYRON'S WORKS FIRST APPEARED

PART III

PRIVATELY PRINTED AND SUPPRESSED EDITIONS OF BYRON'S WORKS

FRANCIS LEWIS RANDOLPH
1951 - 1974

To gather a fine private library has long been a favorite Philadelphia avocation: it predates even dancing at the Assembly Ball or sculling on the Schuylkill. It goes back, indeed, almost to the very founding of the city, when William Penn's friend and secretary, James Logan, brought together the largest private library in the American colonies. That renowned collection still exists virtually intact, an eternal witness to James Logan's passion for books.

With so sterling an example to lead the way, it is small wonder that scores of Philadelphians have formed notable collections. Probably the first American bibliophile in the modern sense — to collect books not only for their literary importance but for rarity and beauty as well — was a Philadelphian born and bred: William Mackenzie (1758-1828). Among his 7,000 volumes was a Caxton and three printed by Wynkyn de Worde (perhaps the only examples in the United States at the time), very early editions of Dante and Chaucer, Jenson's *Pliny*, Venice 1476, on vellum; and some thirty other books printed before 1500 — five of them, to this day, the only copies in America!

A generation later, and you find James Cox, shabby in attire, diffident in mien, and a lone wolf as a collector, buying a copy of Keats' *Poems* (1817) soon after it was published — quite possibly the first American to do so. Toward the end of the century, there was Harold Pierce, whose shelves were radiant with a complete set of Kelmscott Press books *on vellum*, purchased directly from the printer himself — William Morris.

Such admirable sensitivity to both the content and format of books was the hallmark of many a local bibliophile. There come to mind, for instance, Morris Parrish and row upon row of scarce Victorian novels in superb condition, Ellis Ames Ballard and his Kipling first editions, Harry Elkins Widener and breathtaking Elizabethan rarities, his kinsman William I. Elkins' glittering array of Dickens presentation copies, Col. Richard Gimbel with matchless Poe and Paine treasures, Penrose Hoopes' little known but extremely important gathering of early scientific works, Moncure Biddle's very comprehensive material on the Latin poet Horace, Lessing J. Rosenwald's world-famous collection of illustrated books.

The most widely known of all Philadelphia bibliophiles are, of course, A. Edward Newton and Dr. A.S.W. Rosenbach. Newton's own books on collecting delighted readers throughout the English-speaking world. Dr. Rosenbach's spectacular purchases at auction sent everyone to the attic in hopes of finding a Gutenberg Bible or a First Folio in some cobwebbed trunk. Moreover, both possessed a highly individual personality, that indefinable something which fascinated their contemporaries and has made legends of them ever since. They hold a very special place in the annals of Philadelphia, from any point of view.

And yet I do not hesitate to suggest that another Philadelphia collector, had he been granted an equal life span, would have won for himself a niche beside Newton and Dr. Rosenbach. I refer to Francis Lewis Randolph, who died in 1974, aged twenty-two.

Francis Lewis Randolph was born on June 17, 1951 in Bryn Mawr, Pennsylvania, the son of Evan and Frances Randolph. I have not the slightest doubt that every detail of the occasion had been prearranged by Frank himself. June, the loveliest month of the year; Bryn Mawr, the most erudite of suburbs; Evan and Frances, loving and understanding parents — all chosen with a fastidiousness rare in the newborn but completely characteristic of Frank Randolph.

For one who displayed such sure taste so early, it is rather surprising that Frank began his career as a collector so late in life. He was, in fact, all of nine years old when he decided to collect ancient Egyptian artifacts. Not stamps, not cigar-bands, not baseball cards: *ancient Egyptian artifacts.* He was soon utterly absorbed in the subject, on familiar terms with every Pharoah, and could reel off entire dynasties by heart. He journeyed to New York to visit a dealer of whom he had bought various items by mail; I surmise that the dealer, confronted for the first time in person by this incredibly youthful and knowledgeable customer, could not have been more unnerved had King Tutankhamen himself walked into the shop.

The interest in ancient civilizations steadily deepened. At fourteen, Frank was no longer content to find artifacts in dealers' shops; he joined an archeological expedition in Italy and spent a blissful summer sifting through the centuries for Etruscan shards *in situ.*

Fascinated though Frank was by the remote past, he was equally preoccupied with the immediate present. Pharoahs and Greek philosophers and Roman emperors were all nice people to know, and it was great fun to dig up the utensils that once contained their nectar and ambrosia; but modern man required sustenance too. So one always went to Frank's parties with a special anticipation. For this was a host whose own wizardry in the kitchen brought forth the most delicious and exotic dinners; who, as a birthday present to himself, printed a handsome brochure of original recipes:

> "Prepare and coarsely chop one pound of chestnuts. Add one cup pot-style cottage cheese, riced; salt, white pepper, butter, 1/2 cup cream, two large shallots, chopped; an egg, one ounce Madeira, ginger and allspice. Use as stuffing in chicken."

One can only envy the chicken.

I suppose I need hardly add that some of the most ravishing wines in the world graced Frank's table. Whether there has ever been an infant prodigy wine connoisseur, I do not know; but the fact remains that Frank as a schoolboy possessed a small cellar, every bottle chosen by himself, which would have impressed the sommeliers at the Tour d'Argent. And I wonder if any other teen-ager ever had the temerity to invite a local group of *Chevaliers du Tastevin* to dine at his house — and to emerge from that supreme test amid the bravos of his awed guests.

Young people so totally dedicated to special fields of interest often chafe at the constraints of formal schooling.

Nonetheless, at Milton Academy Frank was graduated with honors. He had been president of its Art Club, vice-president of the Historical and Dramatic Societies; on the boards of *The Milton Review*, the school magazine, and the Literary Society; a member of the debating team, director of the annual school play; and, for good measure, manager of the tennis and wrestling teams. He himself was not permitted to participate actively in athletic contests. A lamentable accident, when Frank was six years old, had destroyed the sight of one eye, and any risk of further injury could not be chanced. He accepted this blow of fate stoically, seldom spoke of it to others, and in fact few people, outside of his family, were even aware that Frank did not possess normal vision.

Collectors are a notoriously gregarious lot. There is nothing they love more than to talk shop with anyone who shares their enthusiasms; lifelong friendships have often resulted. Congenial by temperament and always genuinely interested in the treasures of fellow-collectors, Frank had a very wide circle of friends indeed. The closest friend of all was Lord Byron.

Never mind that they were never formally introduced. Never mind that Byron died in 1824 and Frank was born in 1951. That is merely a matter of chronology and has nothing to do with spiritual affinities. From early childhood, Frank had been an omnivorous reader; he discovered for himself such flavorsome snacks as the essays of Walter Pater and the short stories of Saki; but the great moment of his life was coming upon the poetry of Lord Byron. Soon afterward, at a friend's house, Frank was allowed to sit at Byron's own writing-desk and hold in his eager hands a manuscript corrected in the poet's handwriting. That did it. From that moment, Byron and he were inseparable.

Byron is of course a titan in literature, the subject of countless biographies and critical studies. Frank, having devoured them all at a gulp, made up his mind to bring together a truly distinguished collection of Byroniana. Reader, do you have any comprehension of the task this fifteen-year-old set for himself? Alexander the Great, who while still in diapers thought it might be interesting to conquer the world, would have understood and applauded.

But ordinary mortals like myself blanched; we knew the dragons that Frank was sure to encounter in his quest.

Byron is one of the most difficult of all authors to collect. It is not simply that many of his first editions are now extremely hard to find and very expensive when found. The real problem is that they are fiendishly beset with all sorts of bibliographical pitfalls. A volume might indeed be the first edition — but is it the *first issue* of the first edition? For example, does the word *"shall"* in line 6 of Page 35 lack the final *"l"*? And is Page 179 misnumbered *"79"*? Is the errata leaf present? The binding: is it the *earliest* state of the printed wrappers? Or the second state, with the date corrected in the publisher's imprint? And, ah, yes, does the volume contain the *earliest* advertisements, or those inserted later?

Faced with such hazards, the sensible would-be Byron collector either decides to pursue a less formidable author or turns to gardening. But one who could take the loss of an eye in stride could meet this challenge too. If Byron's first editions were expensive, one could earn money working all summer as a chef on a Maine estate. One could forego new clothes and wear instead great-grandfather's still sturdy tweeds. One could sell works of art so impeccably chosen that their value had increased fivefold within a few years. One could even, if sufficiently tempted by a bit of Byroniana, part with some of the ancient Egyptian artifacts: it was not that Frank loved Rameses II less but that he loved Byron more.

Thus, within a remarkably short time, Frank did bring together a superb Byron collection. He had also somehow found time to establish the Byron Society of America, to serve as its president, and to publish its *Journal.* He not only edited the periodical but also designed its handsome format, so redolent of the Regency era.

Probably nowhere else on this continent was the 150th anniversary of Byron's death more notably commemorated than in Philadelphia. Frank organized for the occasion a magnificent exhibition of Byroniana at the University of Pennsylvania, incorporating his own collection and the University's Meyer Davis, Jr. Byron Collection. (He was, incidentally, the youngest person ever elected to the University's Library Council; he was also the youngest ever to serve on the Rare Book Committee of the Free Library of

Philadelphia.) And, by some sorcery or other, he persuaded a group of sponsors to round off the occasion with a dinner-dance in the ballroom of the Academy of Music, with Meyer Davis's orchestra on hand for this revelry by night. Among the patrons, as I remember it, were the Earl of Bessborough, the Earl of Cromer, the Earl of Lytton and the Hellenic Ambassador to the United States. Frank never did anything by halves.

He attended Swarthmore and Princeton but made little effort to excel in his studies there. He was instead devoting every minute to a long-cherished project: the compilation of a new and really comprehensive Byron bibliography. He worked tirelessly on this thorny and thankless task; he had a premonition that there might not be time for anything else. Tragically, there was not even time to complete the enterprise itself. Nonetheless, though the work remains unfinished and unrevised by Frank, all future Byron collectors and admirers will be grateful for its many illuminating and helpful observations.

A signal honor came to Frank in the spring of 1974. He was invited, as an eminent American authority on Byron, to be the guest of the Greek government and to speak at the ceremony marking the 150th anniversary of the poet's death at Missolonghi, Greece, in April of 1824. On April 21 he left Philadelphia for New York and the flight to Athens. It came as a numbing shock, next day, to hear that, on the flight across the Atlantic, Frank had died of a sudden respiratory failure.

We who were his friends tried to derive whatever solace we could from the thought that Frank was not alone when the plane landed in Athens; that, somehow, Byron knew and was surely waiting there to embrace this most devoted of disciples, this kindred spirit.

Seymour Adelman

PREFACE

To varying degrees, previously published Byron bibliographies have been either incomplete, biased or somewhat mistaken. The Byron bibliography most used over the past forty years is that of T.J. Wise — and this work is not only woefully one-sided but also often utterly arbitrary. But there are two facts that give the present bibliography the possibility of being more correct and comprehensive than those published before it. The first is that, though based on the Albè Library, my own collection of Byron first editions, this bibliography is not a catalogue of any one collection or of any one exhibition — it reflects the contents of a number of collections, public and private. Secondly, various bibliographical aids, such as the Hinman Collator, were not available until recently and these aids have proved invaluable in increasing the correctness of this work. It is hoped that this volume may not only impartially rectify the errors in various already published bibliographies, but also, to some degree, illuminate the subject with new discoveries, and serve libraries, collectors and dealers as a reference that is as straightforward, concise and correct as is currently possible.

This work, like Gaul, is divided into three parts. The first treats the published first and later editions of Byron's works, the second lists volumes primarily written or edited by others in which works by Byron were first published, and the third section details the privately printed and suppressed Byron editions. The various editions within their appropriate sections are listed in chronological order. They are described in original condition, as issued, except in the rare instances — indicated with an asterisk — where only rebound copies are known. I have generally avoided detailing advertisement leaves unless they form an integral part of a signature of the book, or where distinguishing marks between one and another issue or variant are among the ads. With the variability of inserted advertisements, I consider it unwise to catalogue, dogmatically, any one leaf or leaves of advertisements with a text, unless, as I have mentioned, those ads form part of the actual register. On the matter of wrappers, it is understood that they are unprinted and lined with white, unless noted. As to boards, in many instances a volume described as being issued in drab brown paper boards often appeared, quite legitimately, at the same time in slate blue boards with tan paper back strip. There is no chronological precedence between these two variant bindings.

I feel a few preliminary words are necessary here on the binding practices of Byron's time. The printed sheets were sent from the printer to the binder to be folded, sewn and put into wrappers or boards. It is quite possible that the first sheets off the press could well have been the last sheets bound, as the binder would have bound the sheets that first had come to hand, with little or no regard for what we retrospectively call variants. And I would hasten to point out that what to us is a variant of the first edition of, say, MANFRED was to the binder a variant of one signature of the group of signatures he was binding together to make that edition of MANFRED. We can judge, in most cases, which sheets came off the presses first, but in a publication of more than one sheet there is no guarantee that the binder would have bound an early printing of signature A with an equally early printing of signature B. In a case such as the first edition of CHILDE HAROLD'S PILGRIMAGE—CANTO IV, where there are seven variations in the printing of separate sheets, and thus 49 possible combinations of the variations (i.e. possibly 49 variants of this first edition), one can only say for sure that any one copy contains a certain printing of a signature. Thus, in many cases, it would be a fallacy to call any one copy of a book, simply because it contains a certain printing of one particular signature, this or that variant or issue of such and such edition of the particular book — one can only say, fortunately or unfortunately, that it is a copy of the first edition with a particular signature in "x" state.

I have only catalogued in detail the first three editions of each work that had more than one edition, unless, as in the case of, say, LARA where an edition following the third contains a key alteration of text or form. There are, following the entries for the first three editions, notes and abbreviated pagination of the later editions.

In cases where there are multiple issues or variants of a volume that share identical paginations I have given one pagination for the two (or more) and pointed out the internal minute differences in both the note section preceding the entry and in the individual entry itself. These note sections preceding the various entries contain summaries of the variants and issues of each edition while the entries themselves detail the "points" of the variants or issues themselves.

In conclusion, I would like to add that I have seen every volume described in this work personally, and that this volume is intended to be the first in a series of three. The second work will treat Byroniana — those works on or about Byron but not written by him. The third will be a catalogue of American, foreign and translated editions of Byron's works.

Francis Lewis Randolph

The Albè Library
Philadelphia

ABBREVIATIONS

Wise or W. — Wise, T.J., A BIBLIOGRAPHY OF THE WRITINGS IN VERSE AND PROSE OF GEORGE GORDON NOEL, BARON BYRON, Privately Printed, London, 1932-33.

Metzdorf — Metzdorf, R.F., A BIBLIOGRAPHICAL CATALOGUE OF THE BOOKS AND MANUSCRIPTS COLLECTED BY CHAUNCEY BREWSTER TINKER, New Haven, 1952.

Texas — Griffith, R.H. and Jones, H.M., A DESCRIPTIVE CATALOGUE OF AN EXHIBITION OF MANUSCRIPTS AND FIRST EDITIONS OF LORD BYRON, Austin, 1924.

Poetry or P. — THE WORKS OF LORD BYRON, POETRY, Volume 7, edited by E.H. Coleridge, London, 1904.

Marchand — BYRON'S LETTERS AND JOURNALS, edited by Leslie A. Marchand, Cambridge, 1972.

BIBLIOGRAPHICAL ENTRIES

The entries in this bibliography take the following form:

TITLE.   Date of issue.

City of Publication.   Publisher.   Printer.

Contents: pagination

Binding as issued. (* indicates a rebound copy)

Size.

Comments.

PART I

THE FIRST AND LATER EDITIONS OF BYRON'S WORK

NUMBER OF COPIES OF FIRST EDITIONS

E.B. & S.R. — 1,000
C.H.P. I & II — 500
C.H.P. III — 12,000
C.H.P. IV — 10,000
Giaour — (?) c. 500 - 1,000
B. of A. — (?) c. 1,000 - 2,000
Corsair — (?) c. 1,500 - 2,000
Lara — (?) c. 2,000
Hebrew Melodies — 6,000
S. of C. - P. — 6,000
Poems — 3,056
Prisoner — 6,000
Monody — 750
Lament — 1,000
Manfred — 6,000
Beppo — 500
Mazeppa — 8,000
D.J. I & II — 1,500
D.J. III-V — 1,500
D.J. VI-VIII — 1,500
D.J. IX-XI — 1,500
D.J. XII-XIV — (?) c. 1,500
D.J. XV & XVI — (?) c. 1,500
Marino — 3,573
Sardanapalus — 6,099
Letter — 2,500
A. of B. — (?) c. 1,000
Island — (?) c. 1,000
Werner — (?) c. 1,000
Deformed — 500-600

The figures for *Don Juan* only refer to the large paper copies.

DEDICATIONS

THE DEDICATIONS OF BYRON'S WORKS

HOURS OF IDLENESS — Frederick, Earl of Carlisle
GIAOUR — Samuel Rogers
BRIDE OF ABYDOS — Lord Holland
CORSAIR — Thomas Moore
SIEGE OF CORINTH — John Cam Hobhouse
PARISINA — Scrope B. Davies
CANTO IV, CHILDE HAROLD — John Cam Hobhouse
PROPHECY OF DANTE — Contessa Guiccioli
SARDANAPALUS — Goethe
CAIN — Walter Scott
WERNER — Goethe
DON JUAN, CANTO I — Robert Southey

PART I

SECTION 1 - THROUGH 1815

HOURS OF IDLENESS.

There are two issues of this volume, and there has long raged a controversy as to whether or not the "second issue," or demy quarto copies, are forgeries. At one end of the spectrum of opinion is T.J. Wise, who dogmatically asserts that the second issue of *HOURS OF IDLENESS* is a "lawful impression honestly produced" (W, I, 10). At the other pole is E.H. Coleridge who, with equal sureness, states that the demy octavo copies are "undoubtedly deliberate forgeries" (P, VII, 250). The opinion of Griffith and Jones represents the middle ground—they say simply, commenting on Coleridge's statement, that " 'forgery' is an ugly word" (Texas, 22) and do not give a firm decision one way or the other. I agree with Coleridge's opinion and will try to show why this is, to me, the obvious view to take.

Ridge was the printer and publisher for both *HOURS OF IDLENESS* and *POEMS ORIGINAL AND TRANSLATED*, and as far as the second volume goes, it is fact that he put out both an authorized and unauthorized edition. I find it hard to believe that Byron's *POEMS ORIGINAL AND TRANSLATED* was the only book that Ridge, at a point after the authorized edition had come out, put out in an unauthorized type facsimile for the benefit of his own pocket. On this example alone, which puts Ridge's probity as a publisher out of the question, I feel it safe to assume that the demy octavo copies of *HOURS OF IDLENESS* are parallel to the forged copies of *POEMS ORIGINAL AND TRANSLATED* in being type facsimiles set up for Ridge's sole profit.

Watermarks are always helpful in detecting forgeries. The authorized copies of *POEMS ORIGINAL AND TRANSLATED* are printed on paper watermarked '1805,' whereas the forged copies are printed on paper watermarked with the Salmon mark for 1811. Thus a book with the title page dated 1808 on 1811 paper is obviously a forgery. But it is also instructive to note that Ridge printed the authorized edition in 1808 on paper dated three years before. Both issues of *HOURS OF IDLENESS* are printed on undated paper with similar watermarks of the same manufactory. The absence of dates on these papers renders any firm conclusion impossible, but even if one assumes that these papers were brought together and one was first used in the year of the publication, 1807, on the basis of Ridge's use of a three year old paper in the authorized edition of *POEMS ORIGINAL AND TRANSLATED*, it would have been easily possible for Ridge to use this paper as late as 1810. Thus the similarity of watermarks in the paper used in the two issues of *HOURS OF IDLENESS* does not indicate in any way that these issues were published at close intervals.

There was in 1924 in the William Clark Library in Los Angeles (ref. Texas, 22) a presentation copy of the second issue of *HOURS OF IDLENESS*. This fact does not mean that Byron authorized this issue. If Byron had sent to Ridge for copies of *HOURS OF IDLENESS* to distribute to his Trinity College friends, and was sent copies of the demy octavo type facsimile "second issue" rather than copies of the authorized first issue, I doubt that Byron, who cultivated an image, at the 1807 period, of flippancy toward his works, would necessarily have noticed the small size difference between the first and "second issues." In light of the few readily obvious differences between the two issues of this volume, I do not feel that the existence of a presentation copy of the "second issue" indicates that Byron, tacitly or otherwise, had authorized the printing of this issue.

Finally, there is no proof that Byron either did or did not authorize the second issue of *HOURS OF IDLENESS*. Ridge did, in fact, ask in the fall of 1807 to put out a second printing of *HOURS OF IDLENESS* and was told not to by Byron (see letter Marchand, I, 148, 149). The result of Ridge's request to put out this second printing resulted, on the authorized side, in *POEMS ORIGINAL AND TRANSLATED*. I feel it certain, in light of the above listed information, that Ridge's request for a second printing of *HOURS OF IDLENESS*, being denied by Byron, resulted in the unauthorized printing of the demy octavo second issue. Whether this issue is called a forgery or unauthorized, it should not on the above evidence be included in the canon of proper Byron imprints.

Newark. By and For S. and J. Ridge

Contents: (i) half title, (ii) blank; (iii) title, (iv) blank; (v) - x preface; (xi) - xiii contents, (xiv) 7 line errata; (1) - 67 text of 'Poems,' (68) blank; (69) fly title 'Translations and Imitations,' (70) blank; 71 - 109 text of 'Translations and Imitations,' (110) blank; (111) fly title 'Fugitive Pieces,' (112) blank; 113 - 187 text of 'Fugitive Pieces,' (188) blank. Imprint bottom center p. 187.

Plain dull pink paper boards, no label.

4 3/4 x 7 5/8

Paper watermarked 'I1 1806' with the small 1 sitting on the leg of the large I. Pages 21-22 (D3) are a cancel. Pages 167-168 remain intact. The binding, unquestionably original as issued, is a variant; copies are usually recorded in drab boards, with or without backstrip, and with white paper label. Besides the two errata noted by Wise that are not listed on the Errata page (i.e. page 114, line 4, 'thnnder' and page 181, penultimate line, 'Thc') there is a third unnoticed erratum on page 5, lines 2 and 3, 'where' being printed twice.

Newark. Printed and sold by S. and J. Ridge

The pagination of this, the spurious demy octavo, edition of *HOURS OF IDLENESS*, agrees in all outward particulars with the proper crown octavo described above, excepting that page 171 is misnumbered 71.

Brown drab paper boards with white paper spine label.

5 1/2 x 9

Coleridge (P, VII, 250) offers excellent suggestions as to why this demy octavo type facsimile of *HOURS OF IDLENESS* should be considered a forgery, though no conclusive proof. Wise (W, I, 9) states that "Coleridge was unable to produce the smallest particle of evidence to support his suggestion (that these demy octavo copies are forgeries)" yet Wise produces neither any suggestions nor any evidence why these copies should be considered genuine. As I have tried to outline in the introduction to this entry, I personally feel that there is amply reason to posit, with Coleridge, that these demy octavo copies are, in fact, forgeries and an almost complete lack of reason, saving Wise's dogmatic statement that these copies are "correct," to indicate that they are genuine.

POEMS ORIGINAL AND TRANSLATED.

There are three issues of this volume; the first was authorized, the third a piracy and the second, previously unrecorded, lies somewhere in between the proper and the improper. The proper, authorized, first issue is described first here and has the 'aaid' misspelling on page 115 and stanza 6 is correctly numbered on page 29. The paper is watermarked '1805.'

In a letter to John Murray of February 6, 1814 (Marchand III, 26) Byron says "Master Ridge I have seen, and he owns to having *reprinted* some *sheets,* to make up a few complete remaining copies." This statement, along with his general reputation for forgery, has always been taken as false by bibliographers. The second copy described here proves this statement, on the part of Ridge, as far as it goes, is true. This second issue, not previously recorded, is made up of sheets of the first issue and the third issue, and follows out Ridge's statement to Byron.

Unfortunately, what Ridge did not tell Byron was that in reprinting lacking sheets to make up whole copies he went beyond this and reprinted the whole volume sometime after 1811. These pirated and completely unauthorized copies form the third issue of *POEMS ORIGINAL AND TRANSLATED.*

Though the second issue is neither all authorized nor all pirated, one must assume, because of the tone of the Byron letter quoted above, that as annoyed as Byron was at Ridge, he was aware of the second issue and, at least, did not order Ridge to destroy it as the poet might well have done.

As to rarity, the pirated third issue of *POEMS ORIGINAL AND TRANSLATED* is the most common of the three issues but is still a very scarce item. The proper first issue is extremely rare and in original boards especially so. I know of only one recorded copy of the first issue in original boards. As for the second issue, the copy described below is the only one recorded.

Newark. By and For S. and J. Ridge

Contents: (i) half title, (ii) blank; (leaf bearing an engraving of Harrow as frontispiece); (iii) title, (iv) blank; (v) dedication, (vi) blank; (vii) - ix contents (pages (viii) and (ix) misnumbered (vii) and (viii)), (x) five line errata; (1) - 68 text of 'Poems;' (69) fly title 'Imitations and Translations,' (70) blank; (71) - 108 text of 'Imitations and Translations;' (109) fly title 'Fugitive Pieces,' (110) blank; (111) - 174 text of 'Fugitive Pieces.' Imprint lower center page 174.

Blue - green paper boards with white paper spine label.

4 3/16 x 6 7/8

The first issue. Paper watermarked '1805.' In the footnote, page 115, read 'aaid.' Page 29, stanza 6 numbered correctly. Wise notes (Wise 1, p. 11) "that every copy of (POEMS ORIGINAL AND TRANSLATED) in its original state has pages 151 - 152 in duplicate." My copy, unquestionably in original condition, does not have this duplication.

This volume is extremely rare and there is only one other copy recorded in original boards as issued.

POEMS ORIGINAL AND TRANSLATED   [*1808*] [*1811 on*]

Newark. By and For S. and J. Ridge.

The collation of this, the second, issue agrees in all outward particulars with the first issue described above.

* Full green crushed morocco, extremely elaborately gold tooled with vellum insets. All edges untrimmed.

4 1/4 x 6 7/8

The second issue. Signatures A, B, C, F, G, H, I, K, M, N, O, P, Q, R, S, T, X and Y are the correct 1808 first issue. Signatures D, E, L and U are a reprint made after 1811 as the paper of these signatures is watermarked 'H Salmon/1811.' The signature U here is of six leaves, rather than the usual four, to replace the mutilated signatures U and V of the first issue. 'Said' in the footnote, page 115, is spelled correctly, and the second stanza, page 29, is misnumbered 4 rather than 6. This copy proves that Ridge actually did, as he told Byron, use newly printed sheets in conjunction with sheets from the proper 1808 first issue to make complete copies. The title page in this volume is the correct 1808 form, not the altered 1811 or still later title page used in the third issue.

POEMS ORIGINAL AND TRANSLATED   1811, or later

Newark. By and For S. and J. Ridge.

The collation of this, the third, issue agrees in all outward particulars with the first issue described above.

Drab paper boards with tan paper back strip with green paper spine label.

4 1/4 x 6 7/8

The third issue. Printed on paper watermarked 'H Salmon/1811.' On page 115, in the footnote, "said" is spelled correctly, and on page 29 the second stanza is misnumbered 4 instead of 6. On the title page, which carries the false date 1808, there is no upper serif in the letter "E" of the word "POEMS," the upper line of the upper double rule surrounding the mottoes is broken and in both of the double rules around the mottoes the heavier line is on the bottom. Signature U is composed of six leaves, not the usual four.

ENGLISH BARDS AND SCOTCH REVIEWERS.

There are two variants of this volume. In the earlier variant the first word of line 7, page 5 reads 'Despatch.' This was corrected during the printing and this word reads 'Dispatch' in the second variant. The collation and all other points are the same in both issues.

Certain copies of this book were sold without the prefatory leaf. As a copy presented to Scrope Davies by Byron on March 1st, 1809 has the preface (Texas, p. 22) - and the 'Despatch' reading - I do not agree with Wise that copies without the preface represent the earliest issue, or, for that matter, an issue at all. The fact that certain copies lack the preface renders them incomplete. As the Davies copy indicates that the copies distributed earliest have the preface, the lack of a preface leaf either represents an omission on the part of the binder or indicates that an insufficient number of these leaves were printed to complement the number of sheets to be bound. As Cawthorn was both dishonest and sloppy, both of these explanations are possible. Wise's contention that the copies without the prefatory leaf constitute an issue is incorrect—the two variants differ in the printing of 'dispatch,' and, as noted above, a volume lacking the prefatory leaf is only incomplete.

Though the 'E & P / 1805' watermark indicates a true first edition, Wise's statement that "Copies without watermark ... are spurious" (W, I, 19) is not necessarily correct. It is always possible in a book made up of half sheets to have only the unwatermarked half of the sheets used. An example of this can be seen in Wise's copy of the first issue of *POEMS ORIGINAL AND TRANSLATED,* which he stated was printed on paper without watermark (W, I, 10). His copy did not have a half sheet with the '1805' watermark, only the unwatermarked half of the sheets. This situation may well be true in copies of *ENGLISH BARDS AND SCOTCH REVIEWERS.* If copies with all the proper internal points exist on unwatermarked paper, they may well be part of the proper first edition made up of sheets printed on the unwatermarked half of the half sheets.

ENGLISH BARDS AND SCOTCH REVIEWERS — SPURIOUS EDITIONS

There are many spurious editions of this poem. In the following entries I have described the genuine issues and editions only and have not, as did Wise, listed various of the spurious forms. Thus if any copy of an edition of *ENGLISH BARDS AND SCOTCH REVIEWERS* does not conform to the points of that edition as described below, it may be assumed to be a spurious imprint.

ENGLISH BARDS AND SCOTCH REVIEWERS   *1809 [March]*

London.   Cawthorn.   Collins

Contents: (i) half title, (ii) blank; (iii) title, (iv) Collins imprint between double rules lower center; (v), vi preface; (1) - 54 text - imprint repeated bottom center.

Brown drab paper boards, usually imprinted in black on both sides.

4 3/8 x 7 3/8

This is a copy of the first issue, with the first word, 'Dispatch,' of the seventh line, page five, misspelled 'Despatch.' The following points also indicate the proper first edition. Paper watermarked 'E & P 1805.' Fourth line of preface, third word reads 'Author.' Line 47, page 5, reads 'wizard's.' Line 159, page 14, reads 'crouds.'

ENGLISH BARDS AND SCOTCH REVIEWERS   *1809*

London.   Cawthorn.   Collins.

Contents: as in the first issue.

Brown drab paper boards, imprinted in black on both sides.

4 3/8 x 7 7/16

The second issue with the first word of the seventh line, 'Dispatch,' of page five spelled correctly. The paper is watermarked 'E & P / 1805.'

ENGLISH BARDS AND SCOTCH REVIEWERS   *1809*

London.   Cawthorn.   Deans & Co.

Second Edition

Contents: (i) half title, (ii) blank; (iii) title, (iv) blank with imprint lower center; (v) - vii preface, (viii) blank; (1) - 85 text of the poem, (86) blank with a three line advertisement upper center; (87), - (88) Cawthorn and British Circulating Library advertisement.

Drab brown paper boards without label.

5 1/16 x 7 3/4

The second edition. Printed on paper watermarked 'Budgen & Wilmott /1808.' 'Aberdeen' in line 1007, page 80, is misspelled 'Abedeen,' and on page 22 'crowds' is misspelled 'crouds.' The genuine second edition is scarcer than either the first or third editions.

ENGLISH BARDS AND SCOTCH REVIEWERS   *1810*

London.   Cawthorn.   Collins

Third Edition

Contents: (i) half title, (ii) blank; (iii) title, (iv) blank with imprint lower center between double rules; (v) - vii preface,

(viii) blank; (1) - 82 text of the poem; (83) - 85 postscript, (86) - (88) Cawthorn advertisements, with imprint bottom center page (88).

Drab paper boards with no label.

5 1/8 x 7 3/4

The third edition, as indicated on the title page. On paper watermarked 'Edmeads & Pine/1807,' 'E & P/1804' and 'J Whatman/1805.' The stocks of paper used in this edition may vary from copy to copy. The genuine third edition is scarcer than the first edition, but not as scarce as the second edition.

ENGLISH BARDS AND SCOTCH REVIEWERS

Fourth Editions

There are two fourth editions which are both apparently genuine. In both of these editions, in the first line of the first footnote, page 5, 'ingenuous' is misspelled 'ingenious.'

ENGLISH BARDS AND SCOTCH REVIEWERS   1810

London.   Cawthorn.   Collins.

Contents: (i) half title, (ii) blank; (iii) title, (iv) blank; (v) - vii preface (to the third edition), (viii) blank; (1) - 85 text and postscript of the poem, (86) - (88) Cawthorn advertisements with imprint bottom center page (88).

Brown drab paper boards with white paper spine label.

4 15/16 x 8 1/4

The first fourth edition. The paper has no watermark (Wise notes (W, I, 26) that his copy of the first fourth edition is printed on paper watermarked 'G & R T.')

London.   Cawthorn.   Cox, Son, and Baylis.

Contents: (i) half title, (ii) blank; (iii) title, (iv) blank; (v) - vii preface, (viii) blank; (1) - 85 text of poem and postscript, (86) blank with imprint bottom center.

Drab brown paper boards with white paper spine label.

4 13/16 x 7 11/16

The second fourth edition, on paper watermarked 'J Whatman/1805.'

ENGLISH BARDS AND SCOTCH REVIEWERS

The suppressed fifth edition.

For the pagination and description of this volume, see Part III.

There are three states of the first edition of this volume. In the first variant, pages 189-190 (BB3) are uncancelled, and in line 11, page 97 the last two words read "vengeance forego;". It is doubtful if this state was ever issued, as it is almost certain that leaf BB3 was cancelled before publication. This leaf was cancelled so that the title of the poem on page 189 would read "Written beneath a Picture," not "Written beneath a Picture of J--V--D."

In the second variant, which was the first variant to be distributed, leaf BB3 is a cancel and the eleventh line on page 97 reads " ... vengeance forego:". In the third variant, these words are punctuated " ... vengeance forego?".

It is of interest to note that the copy presented by Byron to Hobhouse on March 24, 1812 is the second variant, and the copy presented by Byron to Thomas Campbell on March 19, 1812 is the third variant. Thus it would seem that the change in line 11, page 97 not only occurred during the printing, but that the binder gave neither sheet preference over the other. Both of these presentation copies are in the Tinker Collection.

CHILDE HAROLD'S PILGRIMAGE — CANTOS I AND II
1812, March 10

London.　　Murray, Blackwood and Cumming.　　Davison.

Contents: (i) title, (ii) blank; (iii) - vi preface; (vii) contents, (viii) errata; (1) fly title 'Childe Harold's Pilgrimage./ A Romaunt.', (2) blank; (3) - 58 text of Canto I; (59) fly title 'Canto II', (60) blank; (61) - 109 text of Canto II, (110) blank; (111) fly title 'Notes', (112) blank; (113) - 161 text of notes, (162) blank; (163) fly title 'Poems', (164) blank; (165) - 200 text of poems; (201) fly title 'Appendix', (202) blank; (203) - 226 text of appendix; (227), (228) leaf of advertisements. Imprint bottom left page (228).

Greenish drab paper boards, white spine label.

8 3/4 x 11 1/8

As many as five different stocks of paper were used in this volume and the watermarks vary considerably between copies. This book was published without half title, but as the final leaf of ads is an integral part of the volume and bears the imprint, lack of it renders a copy imperfect. Included in this book is a one leaf facsimile of a Romaic text that is variously placed in the binding of the sheets, but is an integral part of the volume.

CHILDE HAROLD'S PILGRIMAGE — CANTOS I AND II   1812

London.   Murray, Blackwood and Cumming.   Davison.

Second Edition

Contents: (i) half title, (ii) blank; (iii) title, (iv) blank; (v) - ix preface, (x) blank; (xi), xii contents; (xiii) note, (xiv) blank; (1) fly title, (2) note; (3) - 109 text of Cantos I and II, (110) blank; (111) fly title to notes, (112) blank; (113) - 201 text of notes, (202) blank; (203) fly title to poems, (204) blank; (205) - 263 text of various poems, (264) blank; (265) fly title to appendix, (266) blank; (267) - 300 text of appendix, with imprint bottom left page 300.

Brown drab paper boards with tan paper back strip and white paper spine label.

5 3/4 x 8 3/4

The second edition. Six new poems were added to this edition: 1) "Well! thou art happy, and I feel ...," 2) "And art thou dead, as young and fair ...," 3) "If sometimes in the haunts of men ...," 4) "Euthanasia," 5) "On a Cornelian Heart which was broken" and 6) "To a Youthful Friend." A folded facsimile of a Romaic Letter, an integral part of the edition, is bound up in varying places in this volume.

London.   Murray, Blackwood and Cumming.   Davison.

Third Edition

The collation of this, the third, edition agrees with the collation of the second edition except that the leaf carrying pages (xiii), (xiv) was excised.

Dark brown drab paper boards with white paper spine label.

5 11/16 x 8 13/16

The third edition. No new poems were added to this edition. Again, the Romaic facsimile is bound up in varying places.

NOTE ON THE LATER EDITIONS OF
CHILDE HAROLD'S PILGRIMAGE—CANTOS I AND II

The fourth edition agrees with the third edition save that the leaf carrying pages ix, (x) was excised and two leaves numbered ix-xii were pasted to the old leaf's stub. This addition, carrying the text of an addition to the preface, caused the contents leaf (xi), xii to become misnumbered.

The fifth and sixth editions are identical in collation to the fourth edition.

To the seventh edition 10 new poems were added: 1) "To Ianthe" was placed before the text of Canto I and the following poems added to the Poems section: 2) "From the Portuguese," 3) "Impromptu in Reply to a Friend," 4) "To Time," 5) "Translation of a Romaic Love Song," 6) "Origin of Love," 7) "Remember Him," 8) "Lines inscribed upon a Cup formed from a Skull," 9) "Address on the Opening of Drury-Lane Theatre" and 10) "Thou art not false, but thou art fickle ...."

The eighth and ninth editions are identical to the seventh.

The tenth edition carries one additional poem, "On the Death of Sir Peter Parker, Bart ...." The tenth edition is the last edition of *CHILDE HAROLD'S PILGRIMAGE, CANTOS I AND II* to appear as a separate unit.

THE GENUINE REJECTED ADDRESSES.

There are two issues of the first edition of this book. The first issue consists of 130 pages only, and, on the title page, the last two lines of the list of booksellers read: "Martin, Holles-Street, Cavendish-Square; / and Nunn, Great Queen-Street." In the second issue of the first edition 4 pages were inserted at the end, numbered 131-134 and the title page of the first issue was replaced with a new title page, on which the last two lines of the list of booksellers read: "Chapple, Pall-Mall; and Nunn, Great / Queen Street."

This volume, on pages (1) - 3, contains the first publication in book form of Byron's "Address on the opening of the new Drury Lane Theatre" ("In one dread night our city saw ..."). This address first appeared in *The Morning Chronicle*.

THE GENUINE REJECTED ADDRESSES   1812, November

London.   Printed and sold by B. McMillan.

Contents: (1) title page, (ii) blank; (iii) - ix introduction, (x) blank; (1) - 3 text of Byron's poem, (4) blank, (5) - 130 text of various other poems, with imprint bottom left page 130.

Brown drab boards with deep brown backstrip and white paper spine label.

5 1/8 x 7 5/8

The first issue of the first edition, with only 130 pages. On the title page, the last two lines of the list of booksellers read "Martin, Holles-Street, Cavendish-Square; / and Nunn, Great Queen-Street."

London.   Printed and sold by B. McMillan.

The contents of this, the second issue, agree with that of the first issue except that two leaves were added to form pages 131-134.

Brown drab boards with white paper spine label.

5 1/8 x 7 11/16

The second issue of the first edition, with four additional pages, numbered 131-134, inserted at the end. On the title page the last two lines of the list of booksellers read: "Chapple, Pall-Mall; and Nunn, Great/Queen Street."

THE GIAOUR

There are two issues of *THE GIAOUR*, and two variants of the first issue. On May 23, 1813 Byron wrote John Murray to have 12 copies of *THE GIAOUR* struck off for his personal distribution, and these twelve copies form the first issue of this volume. These 12 copies were printed on heavy paper watermarked either 'John Hall / 1805' or 'J Whatman / W. Balston/1809 (or 1810),' and the difference between the first and second variants is to be found in signature (A) which is comprised of the title page and dedication page leaves. In the first variant of the first issue, Byron's name does not appear on the title page. In the second variant of the first issue, signature (A) (without Byron's name on the title page) was discarded and a new signature (A) was used, with Byron's name on the title page. It is my assumption that the signature (A) leaves used in the second variant of the first issue were from the stock of signature (A) leaves printed for the second issue.

The second issue of the first edition of *THE GIAOUR*, while identical in collation and printing to the second variant of the first issue, was printed on paper with no watermark.

Though the privately printed two variants of the first issue should rightly be placed in the Third Section of this work, I include their collation here for the sake of convenience.

THE GIAOUR   *1813, June 5*
                                                      or before
London.   Murray.   Davison.

Contents: (i) half title, (ii) blank; (iii) title, (iv) blank; (v) dedication, (vi) blank; (1) - 41 text with footnotes, (42) imprint middle center between double rules.

Dark drab wrappers with no label.

5 9/16 x 8 11/16

A copy of the first issue, first variant, without Byron's name on the title page. Printed on paper watermarked 'John Hall/1805.'

THE GIAOUR   *1813, June 5*
                                                or before

London.   Murray.   Davison.

The contents agree with that of the first issue, first variant in every particular except that Byron's name appears on the title page.

Dark olive drab wrappers with no label.

5 1/2 x 8 5/8

The second variant of the first issue. Printed, save signature (A), on paper watermarked 'J Whatman/W Balston/1809.' Signature (A) is printed on paper without watermark. Byron's name appears on the title page, and it is my conjecture that this second variant of the first issue is made up of signature (A) taken from the second issue and the rest of the signatures are from the first variant of the first issue.

THE GIAOUR   *1813, June 5*

London.   Murray.   Davison.

The contents agree in every particular with that of the second variant of the first issue.

Brown drab wrappers, no label.

5 5/8 x 8 15/16

The second issue, printed on paper without watermark. Byron's name appears on the title page.

THE GIAOUR   *1813*

London.   Murray.   Davison.

Second Edition

Contents: (i) half title, (ii) blank; (iii) title, (iv) blank; (v) dedication, (vi) blank; (vii), viii advertisement; (1) - 47 text of poem and various notes, (48) blank with imprint between double rules middle center page (48).

Drab brown wrappers with no label.

5 3/4 x 8 7/8

The second edition, with 816 lines of text, and the advertisement added before the text.

THE GIAOUR   *1813*

London.   Murray.   Davison.

Third Edition

Contents: (i) half title, (ii) blank; (iii) title, (iv) blank; (v) dedication, (vi) blank; (vii), viii advertisement; (1) - 53 text of the poem and various prose notes, (54) - (56) Murray advertisements, with imprint bottom left page (56).

Dark brown drab wrappers with no label.

5 3/4 x 8 13/16

The third edition. There are two variants of this edition; in one page (ii) is blank and in the other page (ii) carries an advertisement for Mme. de Stael's *De L'Allemagne.* The number of lines of the poem printed in this edition is 950.

NOTE ON THE LATER EDITIONS OF *THE GIAOUR*

In the fourth edition of *THE GIAOUR* 1048 lines were printed. The abbreviated pagination is: viii and (56). The last three pages are occupied with Murray advertisements.

The fifth edition of *THE GIAOUR* carries 1215 lines and its abbreviated pagination is vii and (68). There are two variants of this edition, one with pages (67), (68) blank with the imprint between double rules middle center page (68), and another where pages (67), (68) are occupied by Murray advertisements.

The sixth edition is identical to the fifth.

The seventh edition is comprised of 1334 lines and its abbreviated pagination is: viii and (76).

The eighth, ninth, tenth, eleventh and twelfth editions of *THE GIAOUR* agree with the seventh in collation and content.

There are two issues of *THE BRIDE OF ABYDOS*, and two variants of the first issue. In both variants of the first issue there are 20 lines on page 47. In the first variant of the first issue there is no errata slip. In the second variant of this issue there is a two item errata slip. It is surmised that the first variant exists because a number of copies of the first issue were distributed before the items mentioned in the errata slip were noticed and the slip printed. The first variant of the first issue is not hypothetical, as is the first variant of the first edition of *CHILDE HAROLD'S PILGRIMAGE, CANTOS I AND II*, as I have a copy in contemporary binding with no evidence of the errata slip ever having been included. Thomas Thorpe has also noted the existence of this variant.

The second issue has no errata slip, and the two items mentioned on this slip have been corrected. Page 47 has 22 lines.

The paper throughout both issues is watermarked either 'W Balston/1812' or 'W Balston/1813.' The errata slip in the second variant of the first issue is usually bound between pages (iv) and (1).

THE BRIDE OF ABYDOS   1813, November 29

London.   Murray.   Davison.

Contents: (i) title, (ii) blank; (iii) dedication, (iv) blank; (1) - 60 text of the poem; (61) - 72 text of the notes with imprint left bottom, page 72.

Brown drab wrappers with no label.

5 11/16 x 8 7/8

The first variant of the first issue. On page 47 there are only 20 lines. There is no errata slip bound up with copies of this variant and this can be explained by their being issued before the errata slip was printed.

THE BRIDE OF ABYDOS   *1813, November 29*

London.   Murray.   Davison.

The contents agree with that of the first variant of the first issue.

Green drab wrappers with no label.

5 3/4 x 9

The second variant of the first issue. There are 20 lines on page 47 and there is an errata slip bound in between pages (iv) and (1).

THE BRIDE OF ABYDOS   *1813, November 29*

London.   Murray.   Davison.

The contents agree with that given for the first variant of the first issue.

Green drab wrappers with no label.

5 13/16 x 9

The second issue without errata slip, the errors having been corrected. Page 47 has 22 lines of text, and on page 60 the eighth line of text on the page is numbered 720. In subsequent editions the sixth line on page 60 is numbered 720.

London.   Murray.   Davison.

Second Edition

The contents of this, the second edition, agree with the contents of the second issue of the first edition.

Brown drab paper wrappers with no label.

5 3/4 x 8 13/16

THE BRIDE OF ABYDOS   1813

London.   Murray.   Davison.

Third Edition

The contents of this, the third edition, agree in all outward particulars with the contents of the second edition.

Light brown drab wrappers with no label.

5 13/16 x 8 11/16

The third edition. Six lines of text were inserted into the text by lengthening certain pages. On page 45, between lines 401 and 402, these six lines were added and on page 43 the number of lines was increased from 20 to 22, on page 45 the number of lines was increased from 22 to 24 and on page 46 again from 22 to 24.

NOTE ON THE LATER EDITIONS OF THE BRIDE OF ABYDOS

The contents of the fourth through eighth editions of THE BRIDE OF ABYDOS all agree with the contents of the second issue of the first edition. In the eighth edition the words 'The End' were added above the imprint on page 72. In the ninth, tenth and eleventh editions the notes were compressed so that they occupy only pages (61) - 71, and the imprint was moved to the center middle of page (72).

THE CORSAIR

On the question of the issues and variants of the first four editions of *THE CORSAIR* I find it necessary, and most certainly correct, to agree with the interpretation of Mr. Robert F. Metzdorf rather than with that of Wise. Mr. Metzdorf's conclusions are correct, if incomplete, whereas Wise's are fantastic.

There were four sets of printed sheets made for the early editions of *THE CORSAIR* and various combinations of these sheets with different title pages and in various differing states of alteration make up all the early variants and issues. Set A, the first printed, was composed of xii and 108 pages. The imprint of set A is at the bottom of page 108. Set A is to be found complete (the first issue) and with the last eight pages excised (the second issue). Then set B was printed and consisted of xii and 100 pages, with the imprint at the foot of page 100. This was issued first alone (the third issue) and then (the fourth issue) with set C. Set C consists of eight pages, numbered (101) - 108, with the imprint at the foot of page 108. Finally set D was printed, which is identical to set A except for the title page, *i.e.* xii and 108 pages with imprint only at the bottom of page 108.

THE CORSAIR.

As is noted below, at least the first four editions of *THE CORSAIR* were ready to be sold on the day of publication, February 1, 1814. For this reason I use the term issue in the entries below in a guarded sense, as all of these various 'issues' were issued on the same day. Thus when I describe one volume as a 'first issue' or a 'second issue' I mean that the sheets of the so-called 'first issue' were printed before the sheets of the 'second issue.'

THE CORSAIR   *1814, February 1*

London.   Murray.   Davison.

Contents: (i) half title, (ii) blank; (iii) title, (iv) blank; (v) - xi
dedication, (xii) blank; (1) - 95 text of poem, (96) blank; (97) -
100 notes; (101) - 108 text of various poems with imprint
bottom left page 108.

Brown drab wrappers with no label.

5 3/4 x 9

First edition, first issue, Watermarked 'W Balston/1812' and 'W
Balston/1813.'

THE CORSAIR   *1814, February 1*

London.   Murray.   Davison.

Contents: (i) half title, (ii) blank; (iii) title, (iv) blank; (v) - xi
dedication, (xii) blank; (1) - 95 text of poem, (96) blank; (97) -
100 notes.

Brown drab wrappers, no label.

5 11/16 x 9

With the W Balston watermark for 1812 and 1813. There is no imprint on
page 100.

First edition, second issue.

THE CORSAIR   *1814, February1*

London.   Murray.   Davison.

The contents of this, the third, issue agree in all particulars, save the imprint on page 100, with that of the second issue described above.

Brown drab wrappers with no label.

5 13/16 x 9

First edition, third issue, the "The End" and the imprint on page 100. The paper is watermarked 'W Balston/1812.'

THE CORSAIR   1814, February 1

London.   Murray.   Davison.

Contents: (i) half title, (ii) blank; (iii) title, (iv) blank; (v) - xi dedication, (xii) blank; (1) - 95 text of the poem, (96) blank; (97) - 100 notes with "The End" and imprint (lower left) on page 100; (101) - 108 text of various poems, with imprint bottom left page 108.

Brown drab wrappers, with no label.

5 3/4 x 8 15/16

First edition, fourth issue, with imprints on pages 100 and 108. Paper watermarked 'W Balston/1813.'

THE CORSAIR — THE SECOND, THIRD AND FOURTH EDITIONS.

Murray told Byron in a letter dated February 3, 1814 "I sold, on the day of publication (February 1, 1814), —a thing perfectly unprecedented — 10,000 copies (of THE COR-SAIR]...." It is obvious that these 10,000 copies were not all of the first edition (of the first six editions of THE CORSAIR

23,575 copies were printed) and as I have seen a copy of the fourth edition with the original purchaser's signature and the date February 2, 1814 on the end paper, I feel it safe to assume that at least the first four editions of THE CORSAIR were included in these 10,000 copies. All of the combinations of the sets of sheets described in the note preceding the entries for the first edition of THE CORSAIR occur in the second, third and fourth editions, in various combinations.

The reason for the large number of variants of the first few editions of THE CORSAIR is the inclusion of the poem "To A Lady Weeping." This poem was first printed in The Morning Chronicle for March 1812 without the author's name. Murray was nervous about Byron publishing this poem with THE CORSAIR as the poem had caused a great deal of political furor, and had, without consulting Byron, ordered the final four leaves of assorted poems (including "To A Lady Weeping") excised. Byron heard of this excision, and ordered Murray to replace these four leaves, as he did not wish to appear to be shirking the publication of "To A Lady Weeping" under his name because of the controversy the poem had created.

THE CORSAIR   1814, February 1

London.   Murray.   Davison.

Second Edition, First Issue

The contents of this volume agree with that of the first issue of the first edition.

Brown drab paper wrappers with no label.

5 3/4 x 8 7/8

The second edition, first issue. Except for the addition of the words "The Second Edition" to the title page, this issue is identical to the first issue of the first edition. Printed on paper with the Balston watermark for 1813.

THE CORSAIR   *1814, February 1*

London.   Murray.   Davison.

Second Edition, Second Issue, First Variant.

The contents of this volume agree with that of the second
issue of the first edition.

* Full contemporary blue Russia, extra.

5 5/16 x 8 3/8

The first variant of the second issue of the second edition. Printed on paper
with the Balston watermark for 1813.

THE CORSAIR   *1814, February 1*

London.   Murray.   Davison.

Second Edition, Second Issue, Second Variant

Contents: (i) half title, (ii) blank; (iii) title, (iv) blank; (v) - xi
dedication, (xii) blank; (1) - 95 text of the poem, (96) blank;
(97) - 100 notes; (101) - 108 text of various poems, with imprint bottom left page 108.

* Contemporary full calf, extra.

5 1/4 x 8 9/16

The second variant of the second issue of the second edition. Printed on
paper with the Balston watermark for 1812.

THE CORSAIR   *1814, February 1*

London.   Murray.   Davison.

Second Edition, Third Issue, First Variant

The contents of this volume agree with that of the third issue
of the first edition.

Brown drab wrapper with no label.

5 3/4 x 9

The first variant of the third issue of the second edition. Printed on paper
with the W. Balston watermarks for 1812 and 1813.

THE CORSAIR   *1814, February 1*

London.   Murray.   Davison.

Second Edition, Third Issue, Second Variant

The contents of this volume agree with that of the fourth issue
of the first edition.

* Contemporary quarter roan.

5 3/16 x 8 1/2

The second variant of the third issue of the second edition. Printed on paper
with the Balston watermark for 1813.

THE CORSAIR, THIRD AND FOURTH EDITIONS.

As far as I am aware, the issues and variants of the third
and fourth editions completely parallel the issues and

variants of the second edition. Though I have not seen either a second issue, second variant of the third edition or a first issue of the fourth edition, I must assume that copies do exist of these variations as they do in the second edition. Thus for the contents of the variants and issues of the third and fourth editions of THE CORSAIR, consult the entries for the second edition altering the words "The Second Edition" to "The Third Edition" or "The Fourth Edition."

NOTE ON THE LATER EDITIONS OF THE CORSAIR.

The contents of the fifth and sixth editions agree with the contents of the first issue of the first edition.

The contents of the seventh edition agree with that of the first issue of the first edition in all outward particulars, but an additional note added to the notes section expanded the text of this section so that it occupies almost all of page 100. Four additional lines of the poem were inserted in the text in this edition, but this insertion resulted in no alteration in the contents.

In the eighth edition, a four page note was added to the notes section. Thus the imprint was removed to the lower left hand corner of page 104, and the abbreviated contents of this edition are xii and 112.

The contents of the ninth edition agree with that of the seventh edition.

ODE TO NAPOLEON BUONAPARTE   *1814, April 16*

London.   Murray.   Bulmer.

Contents: (1) half title, (2) blank; (3) title, (4) blank; (5) nine line quote from Gibbon between single rules, (6) blank; (7) - 14 text of poem; (15) seven line ad for Byron's "Poems" with Bulmer imprint lower left, (16) blank.

Brown drab wrappers, printed on the front wrapper.

5 11/16 x 8 3/4

No watermark. Very rare, in any condition—the half title is usually lacking. A copy in wrappers is an extreme rarity.

ODE TO NAPOLEON BUONAPARTE   *1814*

London.   Murray.   Bulmer.

Second Edition

The contents of this, the second, edition agree with that of the first edition.

Drab brown paper wrappers, printed in black on the front cover.

5 3/4 x 8 13/16

The second edition, printed on paper with no watermark.

ODE TO NAPOLEON BUONAPARTE   *1814*

London.   Murray.   Bulmer.

Third Edition

Contents: (1) half title, (2) blank; (3) title, (4) blank; (5) nine line quote from Gibbon between single rules, (6) blank; (7) - 15 text of the poem, with imprint bottom left page 15, (16) blank.

Brown drab wrappers printed in black on the front wrapper.

5 7/8 x 8 15/16

The third edition. Because of the tax, or stamp duty, imposed on publications printed on less than a full sheet, Byron supplied Murray with an additional stanza (placed between stanzas 4 and 5 of the first edition) so that the text of the poem would occupy the full sheet.

NOTE ON THE LATER EDITIONS OF THE *ODE TO NAPOLEON BUONAPARTE.*

Of the first ten editions of the *ODE*, all published in 1814, the first nine were published anonymously and the tenth edition was the first to carry Byron's name. There were no changes in the text proper after the third edition.

LARA, A TALE.   JACQUELINE, A TALE

There are four variants in the first edition of these poems. These variants have to do with the paper used and with falling type, so even though they do not reflect anything of importance concerning the poems themselves, they do indicate an order of printing.

The two stocks of paper used are as follows; the first has no watermark and is noticably thinner and less bulky than the second stock, which is watermarked 'J/1808' or 'J B/1808.' Griffith and Jones refer to copies printed on this heavier stock as "First edition on fine paper." To avoid any ambiguity, I would point out that though these copies are both "first edition" and "on fine paper," there is no evidence that there was any specially produced "edition on fine paper," *i.e.* the finer stock was used simply because it was at hand, not to create a "fine paper edition" per se.

During the course of printing this volume, in two separate instances type either fell or became crooked. First the roman two in Canto II in the running title at the top of page 82 was jostled and became askew. Later in the printing the second period in the running title on page 20 fell out of the form and thus there was only one period in that running title.

To encapsulate these slight variations: the first variant was printed on unwatermarked paper, and the two typographical faults mentioned above are not present. These two faults also are not present in the second variant which is printed on heavy watermarked paper, as are the third and fourth variants. In the third variant, the roman numeral two in the running title, page 82, appears askew. In the fourth variant, not only does this fault appear, but the second period in the running title, page 20, has been dropped.

Though it cannot be asserted positively, it would seem that copies of the first variant were issued in blue drab boards with tan paper back strip, and the copies of the later variants were issued in dark brown drab boards.

JACQUELINE, A TALE is the work of Samuel Rogers, and had appeared in a privately printed edition previous to being included in this edition.

LARA, A TALE   JACQUELINE, A TALE   1814, August

London.   Murray.   Davison

Contents: (i) half title 'Poems,' (ii) blank; (iii) title, (iv) blank; (v) - (vi) 'advertisement'; (vii) contents, (viii) eight line 'note'; (1) fly title, (2) blank; (3) - 47 text of Canto I, (48) blank; (49) fly title, (50) blank; (51) - 93 text of Canto II, (94) blank; (95) fly title to 'Jacqueline,' (96) five line quote between double rules; (97) - 105 text of Part I, (106) blank; (107) fly title, (108) blank; 109 - 117 text of Part II, (118) blank; (119) fly title, (120) blank; 121 - 128 text of Part III; (129) - (132) Murray ads. Imprint bottom left page (132).

Slate blue paper boards with tan back strip, white paper spine label.

4 1/4 x 6 3/4

The first variant, on thin paper without watermark.

LARA, A TALE   JACQUELINE, A TALE   1814

London.   Murray.   Davison

The pagination of this, the second variant, agrees completely with the pagination of the first variant.

Dark brown drab paper boards, with white paper spine label.

4 3/16 x 6 11/16

The second variant, printed on thick paper watermarked either 'J/1808' or 'JB/1808.'

LARA, A TALE   JACQUELINE, A TALE   *1814*

London.   Murray.   Davison

The pagination of this, the third variant, agrees completely
with the pagination of the first variant.

Dark brown drab paper boards, with white paper spine label.

4 1/4 x 6 3/4

The third variant, on heavy paper watermarked 'JB/1808.' In the running
title at the top of page 82 the roman numeral II of Canto II is crooked.

LARA, A TALE   JACQUELINE, A TALE   *1814*

London.   Murray.   Davison

The pagination of this, the fourth variant, agrees completely
with the pagination of the first variant.

Dark brown drab paper boards, with white paper spine label.

4 1/4 x 6 13/16

The fourth variant, on thick paper watermarked 'J/1808' and 'JB/1808.' In
the running title at the top of page 82 the roman numeral II of Canto II is
crooked, and the second period in the running title, page 20, has fallen and
as a result there is only one period in this line.

London.   Murray.   Davison.

Second Edition

The pagination of this, the second, edition agrees with that of the first edition.

Dark brown drab paper boards with white spine label.

4 1/4 x 6 3/4

The second edition, printed on paper with no watermark.

LARA, A TALE   JACQUELINE, A TALE   1814

London.   Murray.   Davison.

Third Edition

The pagination of this, the third, edition agrees with that of the first edition.

Slate blue paper boards with tan-green backstrip, white paper spine label.

4 5/16 x 6 11/16

The third edition, printed on paper with no watermark.

LARA, the Fourth and first separate edition.

There are two separate issues of this volume. The first issue ends on page 70, with (71) blank and (72) with the imprint center middle. The second issue was expanded with an additional quarter sheet, numbered 71-74, carrying a prose note. This quarter sheet was inserted between what were in the first issue pages 70 and (71).

All copies of this edition I have seen or that I know of have page 13 misnumbered 31. Copies may exist with page 13 properly numbered, but at this point none has been recorded.

LARA   *1814*

London.   Murray.   Davison.

Contents: (i) half title with imprint lower left, (ii) blank; (iii) title, (iv) blank; (1) fly title 'Canto I,' (2) blank; (3) - 35 text of Canto I, (36) blank; (37) fly title 'Canto II,' (38) blank; (39) - 70 text of Canto II; (71) blank; (72) blank with imprint middle center.

Brown drab wrappers, no label.

5 5/8 x 8 7/8

Paper watermarked 'W. Balston/1814.' This is the first issue of the fourth edition of *LARA*. The first three editions of *LARA* were published with Rogers' *JACQUELINE*, and thus this is the first separate edition of *LARA*. It is also the first edition to bear Byron's name.

LARA   *1814*

London.   Murray.   Davison.

Contents: (i) half title with imprint lower left, (ii) blank; (iii) title, (iv) blank; (1) fly title to Canto I, (2) blank; (3) - 35 text of Canto I, (36) blank; (37) fly title to Canto II, (38) blank; (39) - 70 text of Canto II; (71) - (74) prose note; (75) blank; (76)

blank with imprint middle center.

Brown drab wrappers, with no label.

5 11/16 x 8 7/8

Paper watermarked 'W Balston/1814.' The second issue of the fourth and
first separate edition with pages (71) - (74) inserted.

1814, December 1

London.   Murray.   No printer indicated.

It was announced in the advertisements at the end of the first edition of LARA (published in August, 1814) that "A complete Set of Plates, illustrative of Lord Byron's Works, is in great forwardness, to be engraved by HEATH from the original Designs of STOTHARD." A set of 12 plates was published by Murray on December 1st, 1814 (even though 13 plates were mentioned in the advertisements that form part of the first edition of HEBREW MELODIES, only 12 were issued) in four styles: quarto proofs on india paper at three guineas, quarto proofs at two guineas, in octavo size at one pound ten and in small octavo at 18 shillings. All of the designs of these plates were done by Thomas Stothard, R.A., but were engraved by several artists. Four plates illustrate CHILDE HAROLD'S PILGRIMAGE and there are two illustrations each for THE GIAOUR, THE BRIDE OF ABYDOS, THE CORSAIR and LARA. Though these plates are not true first editions, from the literary sense, they, like Hobhouse's HISTORICAL ILLUSTRATIONS OF THE FOURTH CANTO OF CHILDE HAROLD, are so closely allied to the text they illustrate and in that they were authorized Murray-Byron publications, I feel it legitimate to include them here as opposed to omitting them as Byroniana.

As mentioned above, all plates are based on Stothard's designs. The following list of the 12 plates list them in order and by engraver and the lines they illustrate.

PLATES ILLUSTRATIVE OF LORD BYRON'S WORKS.

(For CHILDE HAROLD)
 1) R. Rhodes, Canto I, Stanza 7, lines 1 and 2
 2) F. Engleheart, Canto I, Stanza 81, lines 6, 7, and 8
 3) A. Smith, A.R.A., the first two lines of 'The Maid of Athens'

4) C. Heath, lines 1 and 2, stanza 2, 'Away, Away, ye notes of woe'

(For THE GIAOUR)
5) W. Finden, lines numbered 498 and 499 in the fifth edition
6) W. Finden, lines numbered 668-670 in the fifth edition

(For THE BRIDE OF ABYDOS)
7) C. Heath, lines numbered 294 and 295 in the second edition
8) F. Engleheart, lines numbered 594 and 595 in the second edition

(For THE CORSAIR)
9) S. Noble, lines numbered 820 and 821 in the second edition
10) F. Engleheart, lines numbered 1547 and 1548 in the second edition

(For LARA)
11) R. Rhodes, lines numbered 401-403 in the fourth edition
12) A. Smith, A.R.A., lines numbered 1069 and 1070 in the fourth edition

HEBREW MELODIES

There are two issues of this volume. The point of distinction between these two issues can be found on page (56). In the first issue, the second book mentioned on page (56) is Rogers' *Jacqueline* and the third book mentioned, Campbell's *The Selected Beauties ...* is "in the press." In the second issue the notice of *Jacqueline* is no longer present and *The Selected Beauties ...* is not noted as being "in the press." Needless to say, not only does the lack of this final ad leaf, (55) - (56), render a copy imperfect but it precludes identifying the particular issue.

Murray's edition of HEBREW MELODIES was published on June 22, 1815. In April of the same year, I. Nathan put out a selection of these poems set to music. Though this edition has been said by some to be the true first edition, I have placed it in the second section of this work—WORKS EDITED BY OTHER AUTHORS IN WHICH BYRON'S WORKS FIRST APPEARED—as in the Nathan edition the music is given as much, if not more, importance as the verses.

As to rarity, the second issue of the first edition is considerably more difficult to find than the first issue.

HEBREW MELODIES   1815, June 22

London.   Murray.   Davison.

Contents: (i) half title with imprint lower left, (ii) blank; (iii) title, (iv) blank; (v) five line note, (vi) blank; (vii)-(viii) contents; (1) fly title, (2) blank; (3) - 53 text of poems, (54) blank; (55) - (56) advertisements with imprint lower left. Inserted after page (56) are two sets of half title and title pages to be used in the binding of the octavo editions of Byron's poems into two volumes.

Brown drab wrappers with no label.

5 5/8 x 8 13/16

Paper watermarked with the H. Smith watermark for either 1814 or 1815. In this edition the name Sennacherib in the poem "The Destruction of Sennacherib" is misspelled 'Semnacherib.' The first issue, with an advertisement of Samuel Rogers' *JACQUELINE* on page (56).

HEBREW MELODIES   *1815*

London.   Murray.   Davison.

The pagination of this, the second, issue is identical to that of the first issue described above.

Drab brown wrappers with no label.

The second issue. On page (56) there is no advertisement for Samuel Rogers' *JACQUELINE.* Paper watermarked either 'H Smith/1814' or 'H Smith/1815.'

HEBREW MELODIES   *1815*

London.   Murray.   Davison.

Second Edition

The pagination of this, the second, edition agrees with that of the first edition save that there are no inserted leaves after page (56).

Light brown drab wrappers with no label.

5 11/16 x 8 7/8

The second edition, printed on paper watermarked '1814.'

PART I

SECTION 2 - 1816 - 1930

London.   Murray.   Davison.

Contents: (i) half title, (ii) blank with imprint lower left; (iii) title, (iv) blank; (1) fly title for THE SIEGE, (2) blank; (3) dedication, (4) blank; (5) - (6) advertisement; (7) - 54 text of poem; (55) - 57 notes, (58) blank; (59) fly title for PARISINA, (60) blank; (61) dedication, (62) prefatory note; (63) - 89 text of poem, (90) blank; (91) notes, (92) imprint center middle between double rules.

Dark brown drab wrappers with no label.

5 5/8 x 9

(Mr. Randolph's collection does not include the second or third edition of THE SIEGE OF CORINTH — PARISINA. According to Wise, Vol. 1, p. 107, these editions agree with the first edition in all points, but we have not added any description unless supplied by Mr. Randolph.)

(Ed. note)

POEMS   *1816*

London.   Murray.   Bulmer.

Contents: (1) half title, (2) blank; (3) title, (4) blank; (5) advertisement, (6) blank; (7) contents, (8) blank; (9) - 38 text;
(39) notes, (40) blank.

*Full green calf, gold stamped

5 1/4 x 8 1/4

First edition, first issue, without poem "To Samuel Rogers."

POEMS   *1816*

London.   Murray.   Bulmer.

Contents: (1) half title, (2) blank; (3) title, (4) blank; (5) advertisement, (6) blank; (7) 12 line contents, (8) blank; (9) - 39
text of poems, (40) notes with imprint bottom left.

Issued stabbed without wrappers.

5 9/16 x 8 15/16

The second issue. Printed on unwatermarked paper. The title POEMS. on
the half title appears between double rules.

MONODY ON THE DEATH OF THE RIGHT HONOURABLE R. B. SHERIDAN

There are three states of the first edition of the MONODY. In the first state, the last four lines of the poem occupy page 12 and the first line on page 11 (line 99 of the poem) reads 'To weep.' In the second state the first line, page 11, reads 'To mourn' while the text still extends on to page 12. In the third state, the text on page 11 was compressed to include the four lines previously printed on page 12, page (12) is blank and the reading 'To mourn' remains.

As is usual with Byron's poems issued stabbed without wrappers, a copy uncut and in original condition is a great rarity.

MONODY ON THE DEATH OF THE RIGHT HONOURABLE R. B. SHERIDAN
                                                    1816, September 9

London.   Murray.   Roworth.

Contents: (1) half title, (2) blank with imprint center bottom; (3) title, (4) blank; (5) - 12 text of the poem; (13) - (15) Murray advertisements with imprint bottom left page (15), (16) blank.

Issued stabbed without wrappers.

5 1/2 x 8 3/4

The first state of the first edition, with four lines of text, page 12, and the first line of text, page 11, with the reading "To weep ...." No watermark.

*MONODY ON THE DEATH OF THE HONOURABLE R. B.
SHERIDAN*

1816, September 9

London.   Murray.   Roworth.

The pagination of this, the second, state agrees in all outward
particulars with the first state.

Issued stabbed without wrappers.

5 1/2 x 8 3/4

The second state of the first edition, with four lines of text, page 12, and with
the reading "To mourn ..." in the first line, page 11. No watermark.

*MONODY ON THE DEATH OF THE RIGHT HONOURABLE R.
B. SHERIDAN*

1816, September 9

London.   Murray.   Roworth.

Contents: (1) half title, (2) blank with imprint center bottom;
(3) title, (4) blank; (5) - 11 text of poem, (12) blank; (13) - (15)
Murray advertisements with imprint bottom left page (15),
(16) blank.

Issued stabbed without wrappers.

5 5/8 x 8 15/16

The third state with the reading 'To mourn' line 1, page 11 and the text
occupying 11 pages only. No watermark.

There are two distinct issues of this volume, and two variants of each of these issues. The issues can be differentiated by the title page, and their variants by internal changes.

The motto on the first issue's title page is set in nonpareil type. The capitol L in the word 'Lettre' in the third line of this quotation is directly under the word 'la' in the second line. In the first variant of the first issue, there is no exclamation point at the end of the first line on page 4. In the second variant of the first issue there is an exclamation point at the end of this line.

On the title page of the second issue, the motto is set in a slightly larger, brevier, type face and the capitol L in the word 'Lettre' in the third line appears directly under the letters 'lu' of the word 'celui' in the second line. In the first variant of the second issue (as is true in both variants of the first issue) the second word in the fifth line of the first note on page (67) reads 'Eagle.' In the second variant of this issue this word reads, for the first time correctly, 'Falcon.'

Of these four variants, the second variant of the first issue is the rarest and exists in only three recorded copies. The first variant of the first issue is slightly more common for when Wise wrote of it, he knew of four copies and I have identified seven, including those noted by Wise. The second variant of the second issue is quite rare, while the first variant of this issue is one of the most easily available of Byron's first editions.

Copies of the first issue were printed on an unwatermarked paper. All copies I have seen or that are recorded of the second issue are printed on a thicker paper watermarked 1816/G. Though these two stocks of paper cannot be, for certain, counted on as a distinctive mark of the two issues, they appear to be consistently used in their respective issues. As the paper used in the second issue copies is the same as the paper used for the PRISONER OF CHILLON, and as Coleridge notes that there is cause to believe that CANTO III was published on Nov. 18, and THE PRISONER on Dec. 5, rather than on the acknowledged date of Nov. 23, and in light of the scarcity of the first issue of CANTO III, I feel it is safe to posit that the copies of the first issue of CANTO III were printed not only earlier, but as a separate unit, perhaps even as a proof.

Note: In certain copies of the second variant of the second issue page 79 is misnumbered 76. This misnumbering appears to have been the result of improperly replaced fallen type and is of no bibliographical importance.

CHILDE HAROLD'S PILGRIMAGE — CANTO III
1816, November 23

London.   Murray.   Davison.

Contents: (i) half title, (ii) advertisement for THE PRISONER OF CHILLON with imprint lower left; (iii) title, (iv) blank; (1) fly title, (2) blank; (3) - 64 text of the poem; (65) fly title to the notes, (66) blank; (67) - 79 text of the notes, with imprint bottom left page 79, (80) a list of the Byron poems published by Murray.

Tan drab wrappers with no label.

5 5/8 x 8 15/16

THE PRISONER OF CHILLON

There are two states of the first edition of this poem, but there is no conclusive proof as to which state came before the other. On the basis of logic, which is, at times, a tenuous concept to apply to bibliography as many of the variations that occur are scarcely "logical," the state below described as state A is presumed to have been issued before the state here called B.

In state A, page (61) is blank and page (62) bears both the Murray list of Byron's poems and the imprint. In state B, page (61) bears the Murray listing and page (62) has only the imprint.

THE PRISONER OF CHILLON   *1816, November 23*

London.   Murray.   Davison.

Contents: (i) half title, (ii) advertisement for CHILDE HAROLD'S PILGRIMAGE - CANTO III with imprint lower left; (iii) title, (iv) blank; (v) contents, (vi) blank; (1) - 2 text of the Sonnet on Chillon; (3) - 22 text of THE PRISONER OF CHILLON; (23) - 53 text of seven poems, (54) blank; (55) - 60 text of notes; (61) blank; (62) list of Murray editions of Byron's poems with imprint bottom left.

Drab wrappers with no label.

5 11/16 x 9 1/16

State A with page (61) blank and the list of poems on page (62). Watermarked "1816/G."

London. Murray. Davison.

Contents: (i) half title, (ii) advertisement for CHILDE HAROLD'S PILGRIMAGE - CANTO III with imprint lower left; (iii) title, (iv) blank; (v) contents, (vi) blank; (1) - 2 text of the Sonnet on Chillon; (3) - 22 text of THE PRISONER OF CHILLON; (23) - 53 text of seven poems; (54) blank; (55) - 60 text of notes; (61) list of Murray editions of Byron's poems, (62) imprint center middle between double rules.

Drab wrappers with no label.

5 5/8 x 9

State B with page (61) bearing the advertisements of Byron's poems and page (62) having the imprint. Watermarked "1816/G."

THE LAMENT OF TASSO   1817, July 17

London.   Murray.   Davison.

Contents: (1) half title - cover, (2) blank with imprint bottom center; (3) title, (4) blank; (5) 14 line note, (6) blank; text of poem (7) - 19, (20) list of Byron poems with imprint bottom left.

Issued stabbed without wrappers.

5 3/4 x 8 7/8

Printed on paper without a watermark. Whether or not Wise's statement that a 'substantial portion' of the original 1000 copies printed were 'wasted' is true or not, this pamphlet is still today a great rarity, especially when the half title-cover is present.

There are two early variants of MANFRED that constitute the first issue. Wise, and others, have called these two variants the first and second issues. In fact, there is no positive way of telling which of these ycelpt first and second issues was issued the first and which the second. In light of this fact, and for the sake of clarity, I will refer to Wise's first issue as the Imprint Variant, as in it the imprint is misplaced, and to Wise's second issue as the Dramatis Personae Variant, for in it the Dramatis Personae listing is, likewise, misplaced. If Wise was correct in calling the Imprint Variant the first issue, it was only because of the fifty-fifty odds. It is just as logical and likely that the Dramatis Personae Variant should be considered the first issue. I personally feel that this is the case, but this ordering is just an opinion, and like any other ordering of variants of the first issue in the case of MANFRED, an opinion that cannot be based on evidence. I will add, for the benefit of fellow collectors, that both of the first two variants of MANFRED are as scarce as the proverbial teeth of hens. I have found the Dramatis Personae Variant to be slightly rarer than the Imprint Variant, but possession of either variant is a true reason for a collector's pride.

In the Dramatis Personae Variant, because two of the page units of type were mispositioned on the larger printing form holding the eight page units of type that print one side of a to-be octavo sheet, the Dramatis Personae listing that should normally have occupied page (5) was printed on page (3), the usual place for the title page. The reverse is true for the title page. It was thus necessary to excise the Dramatis Personae leaf (leaf B2, pages (3), (4)) and replace it in its proper position after the title page. In all copies of the Dramatis Personae Variant, for this reason, the Dramatis Personae leaf appears as a cancel. It is unfortunate that the glue used for this operation was of singularly poor quality and has come down to us as a mucky black residue. The reason for this juxtaposition of these two page units of type is unknown, but can easily be explained. In the printing of the variant, the printer simply mispositioned the page unit of type for the title page in the lower far right hand corner of the wrong form, and vice versa for the page unit of type for the Dramatis Personae page.

In the Imprint Variant, due to a similar mispositioning of a unit of type, the Davison imprint appeared on the normally blank reverse of the title page (page (4)). This misplacement is equally unexplained as are the mispositionings in the Dramatis Personae Variant, as is the reason for this imprint being set up in two lines rather than the usual one. This mistake was later rectified, and the imprint unit of type was returned to its proper position on the reverse of the half title. As both of the mispositionings of units of type that created the Dramatis Personae and Imprint Variants are equally unexplained, it would seem impossible to give either one chronological precedence over the other with any sureness at all. I will give the line of reasoning that has lead me to offer the purely conjectural personal opinion that the Dramatis Personae Variant precedes the Imprint Variant.

The large octavo type form would have had to be opened to correct the mispositioning of either the Imprint or Dramatis Personae type units, no matter which mispositioning came first. As both mispositionings are equally inexplicable, it seems more logical to me that the repositioning of the Dramatis Personae unit of type, being a whole page, might well have engendered the misplacing of the 43 pieces of type that comprise the Imprint. Perhaps these pieces of type were dropped and were not only positioned incorrectly, but also recomposed in the form of two lines. This beside, I feel that the moving of the two whole pages of mispositioned type—the Title and Dramatis Personae page units of type—which is a somewhat major operation, resulted in the misplacement of the Imprint, which is a rather minor mistake. This would mean that the Dramatis Personae Variant occurred first. I feel this more likely than that the moving of the misplaced imprint would have caused two whole pages of type to be mispositioned, a happening that would place the Imprint Variant first. But then, this use of logic may have no place in the often most illogical printing ways of Byron's time. And, I stress again, that, at best, this is only my personal opinion. The graph follows.

MANFRED

Imprint Variant   Dramatis Personae Variant

Half title 1	Imprint 4	Half title 1	4
8	D.P. 5	8	Title 5
7	6	7	6
2	Title 3	Imprint 2	D.P. 3

MANFRED   *1817*

London.   Murray.   Davison.

Contents: (1) half title; (2) at foot: T. Davison, Lombard-Street, Whitefriars, London (in one line of type); (3) title page; (4) blank; (5) dramatis personae (cancel leaf); (6) blank; (7) - 75 text; (76) blank; (77) half title for notes; (78) blank; (79) - 80 notes.

8 1/4 x 5

*modern binding, beige cloth over boards, red morocco spine, gold stamped.

First edition, first (?) issue.

London.   Murray.   Davison.

(1) half title; (2) at foot: T. Davison, Lombard-Street, Whitefriars, London (in one line of type); (3) title page; (4) blank; (5) dramatis personae; (6) blank; (7) - 75 text; (76) half title for notes; (77) blank; (78) - 80 notes.

8 3/4 x 5 1/2

Original brown paper wrappers, uncut.

First edition, third issue.

London.   Murray.   Davison.

Contents: (i) half title, (ii) blank with imprint bottom left; (iii) title, (iv) blank; text of poem pages (1) - 49, (50) blank; (51) blank; (52) imprint in the center of the page between double rules.

Dark brown drab wrappers with no label.

5 7/8 x 8 13/16

I have seen two separate sets of ads bound up with this volume, one 4 pages and one 12 pages, both for Mr. Murray. But as these ads are not part of the volume proper, lack of them does not render a copy imperfect. *BEPPO* is one of the rarest of Byron first editions, especially when the final imprint leaf is present. The paper is watermarked 'E/1816.'

London.   Murray.   Davison.

Contents: (i) half title, (ii) blank; (iii) title, (iv) blank; (1) fly title to Canto I, (2) blank; text of Canto I (3) - 115; notes to Canto I (115), 116; (117) fly title to Canto II, (118) blank; text of Canto II (119) - 227, (228) blank with imprint middle center.

Brown drab boards with white paper spine label.

8 7/8 x 11 7/16

This edition bears neither Byron's nor Murray's names. 150 copies of the original 1500 were destroyed. The paper has no watermark.

MAZEPPA.

There are two issues of MAZEPPA, and in my experience, the first issue is much rarer than the second. In the first issue, the final imprint is on page (70). This imprint was then removed to page (72) and copies with the imprint on page (72) form the second issue.

MAZEPPA.   *1819, July 28*

London.   Murray.   Davison.

Contents: (i) half title, (ii) blank with imprint center bottom; (iii) title, (iv) blank; (1) fly title to MAZEPPA, (2) blank; (3), (4) 'Advertisement' note; (5) - 46 text of MAZEPPA; (47) fly title to the 'Ode,' (48) blank; (49) - 56 text of the 'Ode to Venice'; (57) fly title to 'A Fragment,' (58) blank; (59) - 69 text of 'A Fragment,' (70) blank with imprint center middle; (71) Murray advertisements, (72) blank.

Brown drab wrappers, with no label.

5 5/8 x 8 7/8

The first issue, with the imprint page (70). The paper has no watermark.

MAZEPPA.   *1819, July 28*

London.   Murray.   Davison.

Contents: (i) half title, (ii) blank with imprint center bottom; (iii) title, (iv) blank; (1) fly title to MAZEPPA, (2) blank; (3), (4) 'Advertisement' note; (5) - 46 text of poem; (47) fly title to 'Ode,' (48) blank; (49) - 56 text of 'Ode to Venice'; (57) fly title 'A Fragment,' (58) blank; (59) - 69 text of 'A Fragment,' (70) blank; 71 list of Byron's poems, (72) blank, imprint center middle.

Olive drab wrappers with no label.

5 5/8 x 8 15/16

The second issue with imprint on page (72). Paper has no watermark. The
prose Fragment, begun the same night as Mary Shelley's FRANKENSTEIN,
concerns a mysterious death in Smyrna.

LETTER TO **** ******

I have discovered a cancel leaf in a copy of this volume that has never before been noticed by a bibliographer, and this discovery radically alters the bibliographical profile of this book.

LETTER TO **** ******   *1821, March-April*

London.   Murray.   Davison.

Contents: (1) title, (2) blank with imprint bottom center; (3) - 55 text of LETTER, (56) blank with imprint center middle.

Disbound, preserved in quarter morocco slip-case.

5 5/15 x 8 1/4   (5 1/2 x 8 3/4)

This is a copy of the previously unrecorded second variant of the first issue. Pages 9 - 10, leaf B5, is a cancel. No mention of any cancel in this volume is made by Wise, Metzdorf, or Griffith and Jones. The paper is watermarked 'Balston & Co./1818.'

MARINO FALIERO — PROPHECY OF DANTE

There are two issues of this volume, and two variants of the second issue. In the first issue, the speech of the Doge on page 151 is five and one half lines long. In the second issue, this speech is 11 lines long. In variant A of the second issue, page 101 is misnumbered 110, and in variant B this page is correctly numbered 101. As far as I know, it is impossible to determine if variant A comes before or after variant B chronologically, but I can say with assurance that the variant A, with page 101 misnumbered 110, is a far rarer item than variant B.

MARINO FALIERO - PROPHECY OF DANTE   1821, April 21

London.   Murray.   Davison.

Contents: (i) half title, (ii) blank with imprint center bottom; (iii) title, (iv) blank; (v) contents, (vi) blank; (vii) fly title, (viii) blank; (ix) - xxi preface, (xxii) blank; (1) fly title, (2) blank); (3) dramatis personae, (4) blank; (5) - 167 text of play, (168) blank; (169) - 172 notes; (173) fly title for appendix, (174) blank; (175) - 208 text of appendix; (209) fly title to PROPHECY, (210) blank; (211) dedication, (212) blank; (213) - 215 preface, (216) blank; (217) - 255 text of poem, (256) blank; (257) - 261 notes, (262) blank with imprint middle center; (263) blank, (264) list of Byron's poems.

Light brown drab boards with white paper spine label.

5 5/8 x 8 15/16

The paper has no watermark. The actual collation of the two issues is the same, except for the number of lines on certain pages. There is no extra sheet of ads bound in this copy, nor is an inserted leaf or leaves of ads necessary to make a copy complete.

London.   Murray.   Davison.

Contents: (i) half title, (ii) blank; (iii) title, (iv) blank; (1) fly title to Canto 3, (2) blank; (3) - 64 text of Canto 3; (65) - 67 notes, (68) blank; (69) fly title to Canto 4, (70) blank; (71) - 129 text of Canto 4, (130) blank; (131), 132 notes; (133) fly title to Canto 5, (134) blank; (135) - 214 text of Canto 5; (215) - 218 notes; (219) blank; (220) imprint middle center.

Blue-gray drab boards with white paper spine label.

5 5/8 x 9

There are two variants of this volume. The first has only the word 'Sardanapalus' on the first fly title, page (1). In the second variant this page bears the words 'Sardanapalus/A Tragedy.' Metzdorf noted that "No priority has been established." (CBT, 121). But I have seen a copy of the Sardanapalus alone variant with a contemporary purchaser's signature and date. The date is December 19, 1821, the day of publication. This must mean that this variant was an early one and this inscription certainly suggests that the Sardanapalus alone fly title may well be the earlier of the two. But of course, this evidence, or, it seems, any other can ever be completely conclusive.

SARDANAPALUS — TWO FOSCARI — CAIN   *1821*

London.   Murray.   Davison

Contents: (i) fly title: SARDANAPALUS./ THE TWO FOSCARI./ CAIN., (ii) blank, imprint at bottom of page; (iii) title, (iv) blank; (v) contents, (vi) blank; (vii) - viii, preface; (1) fly title: SARDANAPALUS, (2) note; (3) dramatis personae, (4) blank; (5) - 167, text of SARDANAPALUS, (168) blank; (169) fly title for notes, (170) blank; (171) - 173 notes, (174) blank; (175) fly title: THE TWO FOSCARI ..., (176) blank; (177) dramatis personae, (178) blank; (179) - 301, text of THE TWO FOSCARI, (302) blank; (303) fly title for appendix, (304) blank; (305) - 329, text of appendix, (330) blank; (331) fly title: CAIN, A MYSTERY, (332) blank; (333) dedication to Sir Walter Scott, (334) blank; (335) - 338 preface; (339) dramatis personae, (340) blank; (341) - 349 text of CAIN, (350) blank, imprint center of the page.

Original boards, printed paper spine label, uncut.

9 1/4 x 5 5/8

First edition, variant A.

Note: Mr. Randolph did not have a description of variant B. (Ed.)

Though it has been known for a long time that there are three issues or variants of THE LIBERAL, no bibliographer, to my knowledge, has been aware of these three at the same time. Of the three variants which I call 1, 2 and 3, Coleridge knows of 1 and 2, Wise knew of 1 and 3 and Griffith and Jones of 2 and 3. Of these three variants, 1 and 2 were issued in four parts and the third in two volumes. The third variant was made up by adding new prefatory material to sheets of the first or second variants, and binding up the original four parts into two volumes. Let me stress that the third variant or issue is made up of sheets of the first two variants, except for the prefatory pages, and can thus have the points of the first or second variants, or both.

To decipher the variants of THE LIBERAL the first page to check is the contents page, page (iii), of Volume One. In the first variant there is a 2 item, 4 line errata at the bottom of the page and the reverse is blank. In the second variant this errata contains 4 items and is 6 lines long. The reverse of this page still remains blank. In the third variant the errata list on this page contains 7 items and is 11 lines long. The reverse of the page, page (iv), bears the 'Advertisement to the Second Edition.'

A second point that aids us in distinguishing the first and second issues can be found on page (402), the last page, of the second number of the first volume. This page carries an errata list and in the first variant the last word of the second line of this errata is printed 'realmundone,' i.e. as one word. In the second variant this word is printed 'realmundo ne,' that is with the last two letters separate from the main body of the word. Another point distinguishes the second variant from the first. This is that on the contents page, page (iii) of the first number of the second volume there is a one line erratum in the second variant that was not printed in the first variant.

In the third variant, the 16 pages of signature A of the first number of the first volume were excised and replaced with a signature of 20 pages, which carried in addition the 'Advertisement to the Second Edition' and the preface to the 'Vision of Judgement.'

THE LIBERAL — *VOLUME ONE* — *NUMBER ONE*   1822

London.   By and For John Hunt

Contents: (leaf A1 is completely blank and unprovided for in the pagination); (i) title, (ii) blank; (iii) contents, (iv) blank; (v) - xii preface; (pages 1 and 2 are called for in the pagination, but this is a miscount as this leaf never was present); (3) - 164 text of various pieces.

Red brown drab wrappers, the front wrapper printed in black.

5 1/2 x 8 11/16

First variant.

THE LIBERAL — *VOLUME ONE* — *NUMBER TWO*   1822

London.   John Hunt.   C.H. Reynell

Contents: (165) - 399 text of various pieces, (400) blank; (401) list of the contents of volume one, (402) 7 item, 11 line errata list, imprint bottom center.

Thin brown drab wrappers, the front wrapper printed in black.

5 1/2 x 8 11/16

First variant. Tipped in following page (402) is a slip of 23 lines advertising *The Examiner*. An abbreviated Reynell imprint has been added to the letter press on the front cover.

THE LIBERAL — VOLUME TWO — NUMBER THREE   1823

London.   John Hunt.   Reynell.

Contents: (i) title, (ii)blank with imprint middle center; (iii) contents, (iv) blank; (v) - viii advertisement to the second volume; (1) - 192 text of various pieces - imprint bottom center of page 192.

Red brown drab wrappers, the front wrapper printed in black.

5 1/2 x 8 3/4

First variant.

THE LIBERAL — VOLUME TWO — NUMBER FOUR   1823

London.   John Hunt.   C.H. Reynell.

Contents: (i) blank, (ii) blank; (193) - 377 text of various pieces, (378) blank; (379) list of the contents of number IV, (380) blank with imprint bottom center; (381), (382) leaf of John Hunt advertisements.

Red brown drab wrappers, the front wrapper printed in black.

5 1/2 x 8 3/4

First variant.

There are two variants of WERNER, both of which stemmed from the plan to issue HEAVEN AND EARTH and WERNER in one volume. Because of this plan, the first issue of WERNER bears no imprint at the bottom of page 188. When it was decided to have John Hunt publish HEAVEN AND EARTH in the second number of THE LIBERAL, "The End" and the Davison imprint were added to the bottom of page 188 and copies with these additions form the second issue.

Metzdorf mentions (CBT, 122) that in the Tinker copy of the second issue, pages 153 and 164 are respectively misnumbered 135 and 64. These misnumberings are clearly the result of fallen type, replaced incorrectly or not at all. While I do not think mistakes warrant the naming of another issue, I will say that copies with these misnumberings are rarer than correct copies.

WERNER   *1822, November 23*

London.   Murray.   Davison.

Contents: (i) half title, (ii) blank with imprint bottom center; (iii) title, (iv) blank; (v) dedication, (vi) blank; (vii), (viii) preface; (1) fly title, (2) blank; (3) dramatis personae, (4) blank; (5) - 188 text of the poem.

Brown drab wrappers with no label.

5 3/4 x 8 7/8

The first issue with no imprint at the bottom of page 188. Though the title page bears the date 1823, the actual date of publication was November 23, 1822. The paper has no watermark.

London.   Murray.   Davison.

The pagination of the second issue is identical to that of the first issue except for the addition, at the bottom of page 188, of "The End" and the imprint.

Brown drab wrappers with no label.

5 11/16 x 8 15/16

The second issue with the additions on page 188. The paper here, as in the first issue, has no watermark.

THE AGE OF BRONZE   *1823, April 1*

London.   John Hunt.   C.H. Reynell

Contents: (1) half title, (2) blank with imprint middle center;
(3) title, (4) blank; (5) - 36 text of the poem.

Unlined brown drab wrappers, with no label.

5 3/4 x 9

Paper watermarked either '1822' or 'H. Smith 1818.' There is a sheet of
white, unwatermarked paper set within the wrappers that forms a blank
leaf at the beginning and end of the printed matter.

DON JUAN — CANTOS VI - XVI, (Published by John (and H.L.) Hunt.)

The first editions of the four volumes of the last eleven Cantos of DON JUAN published by John Hunt's firm (i.e. CANTOS VI, VII, and VIII, CANTOS IX, X and XI, CANTOS XII, XIII and XIV—all published in 1823, and CANTOS XV and XVI, 1824) were issued in three sizes: "Large Paper," or demy octavo, "Small Paper," or foolscap octavo, and the "Common Edition," or 18mo (often referred to as 12mo or 16mo). Paradoxically, though the "Small Paper" and "Common" issues of the first editions were printed in larger numbers than the "Large Paper" issues, they are considerably more scarce than the "Large Paper" copies.

EDITION	SIZE	PRICE	NUMBER OF COPIES
CANTOS VI, VII & VIII	Large Paper	9s 6d	1,500
	Small Paper	7s	3,000
	Common	1s	16,000
CANTOS IX, X & XI	Large Paper	9s 6d	1,500
	Small Paper	7s	2,500
	Common	1s	17,000
CANTOS XII, XIII & XIV	Large Paper	9s 6d	There are no figures recorded concerning these editions, but it is assumed that they were printed in numbers comparable to those above.
	Small Paper	7s	
	Common	1s	
CANTOS XV & XVI	Large Paper	9s 6d	
	Small Paper	7s	
	Common	1s	

London.   John Hunt.   C.H. Reynell.

Contents: (i) title, (ii) blank with imprint bottom center; (iii) - vii preface, (viii) blank; (ix) fly title to Cantos VI, (x) blank; (1) - 61 text of Canto VI, (62) blank; (63) fly title to Canto VII, (64) blank; (65) - 108 text of Canto VII; (109) fly title to Canto VIII, (110) blank; (111) - 181 text of Canto VIII, (182) blank; (183), 184 notes; (185), (186) John Hunt ads.

Drab brown boards, with white paper spine label.

5 11/16 x 8 7/8

Paper watermarked 'Balston & Co. / 1822' and 'W. Balston / 1823.' Issued without a half title. This is a Large Paper, or demy octavo, copy.

DON JUAN—CANTOS VI, VII AND VIII   *1823, July 15*

London.   John Hunt.   C.H. Reynell

Contents: (i) title, (ii) blank with imprint bottom center; (iii) - viii preface; (ix) fly title to Canto VI, (x) blank; (1) - 61 text of Canto VI, (62) blank; (63) fly title to Canto VII, (64) blank; (65) - 108 text of Canto VII; (109) fly title to Canto VIII, (110) blank; (111) - 181 text of Canto VIII, (182) blank; (183) and 184 'Notes to Canto VIII'; (185) and (186) 'Publications by John Hunt.'

Drab brown boards, with white paper spine label.

5 1/4 x 7

"Small Paper" or foolscap octavo issue of the first edition. As has been noted, this smaller issue cost less (i.e. 7s as opposed to 9s 6d for the "Large Paper" copies" and was printed in an edition twice the size of the "Large Paper" first editions (i.e. 1500 "Large Paper" and 3000 "Small Paper"). It is presumed that, in light of these facts, more copies were sold of this size, but, paradoxically, it is much scarcer.

London.　　John Hunt.　　C.H. Reynell

Contents: (i) title, (ii) blank with imprint bottom center between single rules; (iii) - vi 'Preface to Cantos VI, VII and VIII'; (7) - 37 text of Canto VI, (38) blank; (39) - 60 text of Canto VII; (61) - 97 text of Canto VIII, with imprint bottom center page 97, (98) blank; (99) and (100) 'Books Published by John Hunt'; (101) and (102) blank.

Issued in very thin brown drab wrappers, unlined, and printed on the upper front cover.

3 1/2 x 5 3/8

The "Common" Edition, printed in huge numbers (this volume in 16,000 copies) according to John Hunt "to prevent piracy." As with the foolscap octavo issue, this "Common" issue is far scarcer than the Large Paper copies of the first edition, for not only were these small volumes not generally preserved in collections, but, due to their highly delicate means of binding—quick sewn and thrown into a very friable wrapper—they usually have literally disintegrated.

London.   John Hunt.   C.H. Reynell.

Contents: (1) half title, (2) blank with imprint bottom center; (3) title; (4) blank; (5) blank, (6) four line note; (7) - 79 text of the poem, (80) blank; (81) - 94 text of appendix; (95), (96) list of John Hunt's publications.

Tan drab wrappers with no label.

5 3/8 x 8 3/4

Paper watermarked '1822.'

London.   John Hunt.   C.H. Reynell.

Contents: (1) title, (2) blank; (3) fly title to Canto IX, (4) blank; (5) - 47 text of Canto IX, (48) blank; (49), 50 notes; (51) fly title to Canto X, (52) blank; (53) - 96 text of Canto X; (97) - 99 notes, (100) blank; (101) fly title to Canto XI, (102) blank; (103) - 148 text of Canto XI; (149) - 151 notes, (152) blank with imprint middle center.

Drab brown boards with white paper spine label.

5 1/2 x 9

The paper is not watermarked. Again, the volume was issued without a half title. "Shakespeare" spelled "Shakspeare" on the title page. A large paper, or demy octavo, copy.

DON JUAN — CANTOS IX, X AND XI   *1823, August 29*

London.   John Hunt.   C.H. Reynell

Contents: (1) title, (2) blank with imprint bottom center between single rules; (3)-24 text of Cantos IX; (25)-47 text of Canto X, (48) blank; (49) - 72 text of Canto XI; (73) -(77) 'Publications By John Hunt,' (78) blank.

Thin drab brown paper wrappers, unlined, printed on the upper front cover.

3 1/2 x 5 3/8

The "Common" Edition. 17,000 copies printed.

DON JUAN — CANTOS XII, XIII AND XIV   1823, December 1

London.   John Hunt.   C.H. Reynell

Contents: (1) title, (2) blank with imprint bottom center; (3) fly title to Canto XII, (4) blank; (5) - 49 text of Canto XII, (50) blank; (51), 52 notes; (53) fly title to Canto XIII, (54) blank; (55) - 110 text of Canto XIII; (111), 112 notes; (113) fly title to Canto XIV, (114) blank; (115) - 166 text of Canto XIV; (167) notes — with imprint bottom center page 168.

Light brown drab boards with white paper spine label.

5 1/2 x 8 7/8

Issued without a half title. "Shakespeare" spelled "Shakspeare" on the title page. A large paper, or demy octavo, copy. Paper watermarked '1822.'

DON JUAN — CANTOS XII, XIII AND XIV 1823, December 17

London.   John Hunt.   C.H. Reynell

Contents: (1) title, (2) blank with imprint bottom center, (3) fly title to Canto XII, (4) blank; (5) - 49 text of Canto XII, (50) blank; (51), 52 'Notes to Canto XII.'; (53) fly title to Canto XIII, (54) blank; (55) - 110 text of Canto XIII; (111) - 113 'Notes to Canto XIII.,' (114) blank; (115) fly title to Canto XIV, (116) blank; (117) - 168 text of Canto XIV; (169), 170 'Notes to Canto XIV; (171), (172) 'Publications By John Hunt.'

Green - grey drab boards with white paper spine label.

4 1/4 x 7 1/8

The "Small Paper," or foolscap octavo, edition. Paper watermarked 'J Whatman / Turkey Mills / 1823.' Issued without half title. It is not known how many copies of this issue of the first edition were printed, but it is assumed that the figure would have been about 2,500 — 3,000.

DON JUAN — CANTOS XII, XIII AND XIV 1823, December 17

London.   John Hunt.   C.H. Reynell

Contents: (1) title, (2) blank with imprint bottom center between single rules; (3) - 25 text of Canto XII, (26) blank; 27 - 55 text of Canto XIII, (56) blank; (57) - 83 text of Canto XIV, (84) blank.

Light drab brown thin wrappers, unlined, printed on the upper front cover.

3 1/2 x 5 3/8

The "Common" edition, issued without half title or ads. Though no figures survive as to how many copies of this issue of the first edition were printed, it is assumed that, as in the recorded "Common" editions, something like 16,000 or 17,000 is the probable figure.

THE DEFORMED TRANSFORMED

There are two variants of THE DEFORMED TRANS-
FORMED. The collation is identical in both. In the first or
signature G variant, signature F (page 81) is mislettered 'G.'
During the course of the printing this mistake was corrected
and signature F reads 'F.' Copies with this reading form the
second, or signature F. variant.

Wise (T.J.W., II, 46) states that the signature F variant is
considerably more rare than the signature G variant. This
may be, but in my experience I have not found it to be so.

THE DEFORMED TRANSFORMED   1824, February 20

London.   J and H.L. Hunt.   C.H. Reynell.

Contents: (1) half title, (2) blank with imprint bottom center;
(3) title, (4) blank; (5) blank, (6) 7 line note; (7) dramatis
personae, (8) blank; (9) - 88 text of the poem, with imprint at
the bottom of page 88.

Brown drab wrappers, with no label.

5 13/16 x 8 13/16

Signature G variant. The paper has no watermark. The wrappers are
unlined, but the body of the text is set within a sheet of blank paper so that a
blank is formed at the beginning and end of the text.

THE DEFORMED TRANSFORMED   1824

London.   J and H.L. Hunt.   C.H. Reynell

Collation identical to the signature G Variant.

Brown drab wrappers, with no label.

5 3/4 x 8 7/8

Signature F variant.

London.   John and H.L. Hunt.   C.H. Reynell

Contents: (1) title, (2) blank with imprint bottom center; (erratum slip inserted); (3) fly title to Canto XV, (4) blank; (5) - 54 text of Canto XV; (55) - 57 notes, (58) blank; (59) fly title to Canto XVI, (60) blank; (61) - 125 text of Canto XVI, (126) three line note middle center; (127) - 129 notes, (130) imprint middle center; (131), (132) Hunt advertisements.

Drab brown boards with white paper spine label.

5 1/2 x 8 7/8

Issued without a half title. Paper watermarked '1822' and 'Balston & Co / 1823.' Large paper, or demy octavo, copy. "Shakespeare" again spelled "Shakspeare" on the title page.

DON JUAN — CANTOS XV AND XVI   *1824, March 26*

London.   John and H.L. Hunt.   C.H. Reynell.

Contents: (1) title, (2) blank with imprint bottom center; (3) fly title to Canto XV, (4) blank; (5) - 54 text of Canto XV; (55) - 57 'Notes to Canto XV,' (58) blank; (59) fly title to Canto XVI, (60) blank; (61) - 125 text of Canto XVI, (126) blank with three line note center middle; (127) - 130 'Notes to Canto XVI' with imprint center bottom page 130; (131), (132) 'Published By John and H.L. Hunt.'

Drab brown boards with white paper spine label.

5 1/4 x 7 1/16

The "Small Paper", or foolscap octavo, issue of the first edition. Though no figures survive, it is probable that 2,500 to 3,000 copies of this issue were printed. Paper watermarked 'J Whatman / Turkey Mills / 1823.'

London.   John and H.L. Hunt.   C.H. Reynell

Contents: (1) title, (2) blank with imprint bottom center between single rules; (3) - 28 text of Canto XV; (29) - 62 text of Canto XVI; (63) - (65) 'Published By John Hunt,' (66) blank.

Very thin drab brown paper wrappers, unlined, printed on the upper front cover.

3 1/2 x 5 3/8

The "Common" edition. No records have survived as to how many copies of this issue of the first edition were printed, but it is generally assumed that, as in the recorded "Common" editions, something like 16,000 or 17,000 copies were printed.

London.   Rodwell and Martin.   Ibotson and Palmer.

Contents: (i) half title, (ii) blank with imprint bottom center; (1) title, (2) blank; (3) contents, (4) blank; (5) - 44 text of the speeches with imprint bottom center page 44; (45), (46) advertisements of Rodwell and Martin publications.

Drab brown wrappers with white paper label on the front wrapper.

5 9/16 x 8 3/4

The paper has no watermark.

Venice, In The Island Of S. Lazero.

Contents: (i) title/cover, (ii) blank; (iii) facsimile of Byron's English and Armenian handwriting, iv - xv, text of various Byron letters mentioning his Armenian studies, with the English text on the even numbered pages and an Armenian translation facing on the odd numbered pages; (xvi) blank; (1) fly title 'Lord Byron's Translations,' (2) - 41 text of various prose translations by Byron, with the Armenian originals on the even pages and the English translations on the odd pages, (42) blank; (43) fly title 'Lord Byron's Poetries,' 44 - 105 text of various of Byron's poems with the originals on the even pages and the Armenian translations on the odd pages, (106) blank; (107) - 233 text of various poems by Pope, Gray, *et al.* with the originals on the even pages and the Armenian translations on the odd pages, (234) blank.

Contemporary (original ?) half dark green morocco and cloth. All edges gilt.

3 3/4 x 6 3/16

The Frank Lester and Laura Mell Pleadwell Copy.

London.   The First Edition Club.   The Curwen Press.

Contents: (i) blank; (ii) colophon; (iii) half title, (iv) blank; (v) title, (vi) imprint top center; (1) fly title to the introduction, (2) blank; (3) - 21 text of the introduction (by Lord Ernle), (22) blank; (23) fly title to THE RAVENNA JOURNAL, (24) blank; (25) - 100 text of THE RAVENNA JOURNAL.

Red and grey print cloth boards with white leather spine label.

5 9/16 x 8 3/4

Printed in black and red on paper with the Ellerslie watermark. Limited to 500 copies, unnumbered.

New York.   Covici, Friede, Inc.   Joh. Enschede.

Contents: (1) half title, (2) blank; (3) title, (4) blank with 'Made in Holland' bottom center; (5) six line note as to the origin of the letters, (6) blank; (7) fly title to the introduction, (8) blank; 9 - 18 text of introduction; (19) fly title to the editor's note, (20) blank; 21 - 24 text of editor's note (by Walter E. Peck); (25) fly title to the LETTERS, (26) blank; 27 - 50 text of the LETTERS; (51), (52) blank; (53) colophon, (54) blank.

Pink paper boards with blue cloth spine printed in silver. Front cover printed in silver.

7 3/8 x 11 1/8

500 numbered copies on Pannekoek papers (with various watermarks), 475 of which were for sale. These letters are generally considered to be spurious.

PART II

WORKS EDITED BY OTHER WRITERS IN WHICH BYRON'S WORKS FIRST APPEARED

ABSTRACT OF THE FIRST PRINTINGS OF BYRON'S SHORTER POEMS.

The following poems were all published first in Thomas Moore's LETTERS AND JOURNALS OF LORD BYRON, WITH NOTICES OF HIS LIFE, John Murray, London, 1830

Fragment - written shortly after the marriage of Miss Chaworth. 1, 56.
The Prayer of Nature. 1, 106.
On Revisiting Harrow. 1, 102.
To My Son. 1, 104
Epistle to a Friend ... 1, 301.
Address Intended to be Recited at the Caledonian Meeting. 1, 559.
"Could I remount the river of my years." 2, 36.
Epistle to Augusta. 2, 38.
On the Bust of Helen by Canova. 2, 61.
"So we'll no more go a-roving." 2, 79.
Sonnet to the Prince Regent. 2, 234.
Stanzas written on the road between Florence and Pisa. 2, 566.
To the Countess of Blessington. 2, 635.
Epigram on an Old Lady. 1, 28.
Epitaph on John Adams. 1, 106.
"Huzza! Hodgson, we are going ... " 1, 230.
"Oh how I wish that an embargo ... " 1, 227.
My Epitaph. 1, 240.
On Moore's last Operatic Farce. 1, 295
"Oh you, who in all names can tickle the town." 1, 401.
On Lord Thurlow's Poems. 1, 396.
To Lord Thurlow. 1, 397.
The Devil's Drive. 1, 471. (Selected stanzas)
Fragment of an Epistle to Thomas Moore. 1, 561.
On Napoleon's Escape From Elba. 1, 611.
Song for the Luddites. 2, 58.
"What are you doing now?" 2, 58.
"To hook the reader ..." 2, 87.
"I read the 'Christabel' ... " 2, 87.
"Dear Doctor, I have read your play, .." 2, 139. (Selected stanzas)
Epistle to Mr. Murray. 2, 156. (Selected stanzas)

On the Birth of John William Rizzo Hoppner. 2, 134.
"Strahan, Tonson, Lintot of the times,." 2, 171.
Epigram. (Rulhieres). 2, 235.
On My Wedding-Day. 2, 294.
Epitaph for William Pitt. 2, 295.
"In digging up your bones, Tom Paine," 2, 295.
"The World is a bundle of hay." 2, 494.
"When a man hath no freedom to fight for at home,." 2, 377.
The Charity Ball. 2, 540.
Epigram on the Brazier's Address. 2, 442.
On My Thirty-third Birthday. 2, 414.
"Who killed John Keats?." 2, 506.
"For Oxford and for Waldegrave ..." 2, 517.
"Beneath Blessington's eyes ..." 2, 635.

───────────

The following poems were all first published in E.H.
Coleridge's THE WORKS OF LORD BYRON - POETRY, John
Murray, London, 1898-1904.

To a Knot of Ungenerous Critics. 1, 213.
Soliloquy of a Bard in the Country. 1, 217.
Translation from Anacreon. 1, 228.
Ossian's Address to the Sun. 1, 229.
Pignus Amoris. 1, 231.
"Oh! well I know your subtle sex ..." 1, 242.
On the eyes of Miss A---- H----. 1, 244.
Egotism. 1, 247.
Queries to the Casuists. 1, 262.
"Breeze of the night in gentler signs ..." 1, 262.
To Harriet. 1, 263.
On the Quotation "And my true faith ..." 3, 65.
Love and Gold. 3, 411.
Julian - A Fragment. 3, 419.
On the Death of the Duke of Dorset. 3, 425.
Venice - A Fragment. 4, 537.
The Duel. 4, 542.
Sonnet on the Nuptials ... 4, 547.
Ode to a Lady whose Lover was killed by a Ball ... 4, 552.
Aristomenes. 4, 566.

The Seventeenth Canto of DON JUAN. 6, 608.
La Revanche. 7, 15.
The Devil's Drive. 7, 21. (Selected stanzas)
On a Royal Visit to the Vaults ... 7, 36.
Ich Dien. 7, 36.
Answer to ----'s professions of Affection. 7, 40
E Nihilo Nihil. 7, 55.
Ballad - to the tune of "Sally in our Alley." 7, 58.
Another Simple Ballad. 7, 61.
Lucietta - A Fragment. 7, 81.
Song of the Suliotes. 7, 83.

The following poems were all first published in R.E.
Prothero's THE WORKS OF LORD BYRON - LETTERS AND
JOURNALS, John Murray, London, 1898-1901.

"Posterity will ne'er survey ..." 17, 246.
Martial. Lib. I Epig. 1. 17, 245.
The Conquest. 17, 246.

The following poems were all first published in Thomas
Medwin's JOURNAL OF THE CONVERSATIONS OF LORD
BYRON, Henry Coburn, London, 1824.

"Remember thee! Remember thee!" 214, (In the first edition
only)
The Irish Avatar. 216 (Complete in the third, or "New"
edition)
Stanzas to the Po. 24
To Penelope. 106
"Behold the blessings of a lucky lot!" 121.
Napoleon's Snuff Box. 235

The following poems were all first published in the London *Morning Chronicle.*

Lines to a Lady Waiting. March 7, 1812.
Address on the Opening of the Drury Lane Theatre. October 12, 1812.
Parenthetical Address. October 23, 1812.
Elegaic Stanzas on the Death of Sir Peter Parker. October 7, 1814.
Ode from the French. March 15, 1816.
Ode to the Framers of the Frame Bill. March 2, 1812.
On this day I complete my Thirty-sixth Year. October 29, 1824.

The following poems were all first published in J. C. Hobhouses's IMITATIONS AND TRANSLATIONS, Longman, Hurst, Rees and Orme, London, 1809.

To a Youthful Friend. 185.
Inscription on the Monument of a favorite Dog. 190.
"Well! thou art happy,.." 192.
The Farewell, to a Lady. 195.
A Love Song. 197.
"There was a time I need not name,.." 200.
"And wilt thou weep when I am low?." 202.
Fill the goblet again! for I never before ..." 204.
" 'Tis done - and shivering in the gale ..." 227.

The following poems were first published as addenda to the first edition of *CHILDE HAROLD'S PILGRIMAGE - CANTOS I AND II,* John Murray, etc., London, 1812.

Lines written in an Album at Malta.
To Florence.
Stanzas composed during a Thunderstorm.

Stanzas written in passing the Ambracian Gulf.
"The Spell is broke, the charm is flown ..."
Written after swimming from Sestos to Abydos.
The Maid of Athens.
Lines written beneath a Picture.
Translation of the Famous Greek War Song.
Translation of the Romaic Song.
On Parting.
"Without a stone to mark the spot ..."
"Away, away, ye notes of Woe!"
"One struggle more and I am free ..."

The following poems were published first as addenda to the second edition of CHILDE HAROLD'S PILGRIMAGE - CANTOS I AND II, John Murray, etc., London, 1812.

Euthanasia.
"And thou art dead, as young and fair ..."
"If sometimes in the haunts of man ..."
On a Carnelian Heart which was broken.

The following poems were all first published as addenda to the seventh edition of CHILDE HAROLD'S PILGRIMAGE - CANTOS I AND II, John Murray, London, 1814.

Lines inscribed on a Cup formed from a Skull.
To Time.
Translation of a Romaic Love Song.
"Thou are not false, but thou art fickle ..."
On being asked what was the 'Origin of Love.'
"Remember him, whom Passion's power ..."
Impromptu, in reply to a Friend.
From the Portuguese.

The following poems all were first published in the London *Examiner*.

On the star of the Legion of Honour. April 7, 1816.
Napoleon's Farewell. July 30, 1815.
"Bright be the place of thy soul!"

The following poems were first published in *Murray's Magazine*, published by John Murray, London

My Boy Hobbie O. March 1887, 292.
Farewell Petition to John Cam Hobhouse. March 1887, 290.
Love and Death. February 1887, 145.
Last Words on Greece. February 1887, 146.

The following poems were published first in the *New Monthly Magazine*.

Lines on hearing Lady Byron was ill. August 1832.
"Could love forever ..." October 1832.
"But once I dared to lift my eyes ..." March 1833.

The following poems were first published in Isaac Nathan's *FUGITIVE PIECES*, etc., Whittaker, Treacher and Co., London, 1829.

"I speak not, I trace not, I breathe not thy name ..." 64.
"They say that hope is happiness ..." 70.
"In the valley of waters ..." 67.

In the case of the following single poems, the title or first line is given first, and then the title of the book in which it was first published.

Farewell to Malta.
POEMS ON HIS DOMESTIC CIRCUMSTANCES, Hone, 1816, sixth edition.

The Curse of Minerva.
POEMS ON HIS DOMESTIC CIRCUMSTANCES, Hone, 1816, eighth edition.

Newstead Abbey.
MEMOIR, Rev. F. Hodgson, 1878. 1, 187.

Monk of Athos.
LIFE OF LORD BYRON, Roden Noel, 1890. 206

Lines in the Traveler's Book at Orchomenus.
TRAVELS IN ITALY, GREECE, etc., H.W. Williams, 1820. 2, 290.

Stanzas to Jesse.
Monthly Literary Recreations, July 1807.

Question and Answer.
Frazer's Magazine, January 1833. 82.

Ossian's Address to the Sun.
Atlantic Monthly, December 1898.

To the Hon. Mrs. George Lamb.
THE TWO DUCHESSES, Vere Foster, 1898. 374.

Condolatory Address.
The Champion, July 31, 1814.

To ----- (G. A. Byron)
Nicnac, March 25, 1823.

"My boat is on the shore ..."
The Traveller, January 8, 1821.

"There's something in a stupid ass ..."
PARODIES, etc., Walter Hamilton, 1888. 105.

"Would you go to the house ..."
MISCELLANEOUS POEMS, Bumpus, 1824.

Windsor Poetics.
THE WORKS OF THE RIGHT HONOURABLE LORD BYRON, Galignani, Paris, 1819. 6, 125.

Endorsement to the Deed of Separation.
THE WORKS OF LORD BYRON IN SIX VOLUMES., John Murray, 1831. 6, 454.

"Yes! wisdom shines in all his mien ..."
CORRESPONDENCE WITH A FRIEND, R.C. Dallas, Galignani, Paris, 1825. 2, 192.

The New Vicar of Bray
THE COMPLETE WORKS OF LORD BYRON, Galignani, Paris, 1831. 116.

Additional Lines to ENGLISH BARDS AND SCOTCH REVIEWERS.
Times Literary Supplement, April 30, 1931.

Verses Written in compliance with a Lady's request, etc.
The Casket, 1829.

Epilogue on Wordsworth's PETER BELL.
Philadelphia Record, December 28, 1891.

———

The following poems were first published in ASTARTE by Ralph Milbanke, Earl of Lovelace, Chiswick Press, London, 1905.

Magdalen.
Harmodia.

ASTARTE (By Ralph, Earl of Lovelace)   1905

London.   Privately Printed at The Chiswick Press.

Contents: (i) half title, (ii) blank; (iii) title, (iv) blank with "All rights reserved" middle center; (v) dedication, (vi) blank; vii - xi preface, (xii) blank; xiii - xxii contents; xxiii list of illustrations, (xxiv) blank; xxv, xxvi corrections and errata; (xxvii) blank; xxviii 16 line note titled "Explanation"; 1 - 94 text of Part One; 95 - 213 text of Part Two, (214) blank; (215) fly title "Appendices," (216) blank; 217 - 337 text of appendices A-L, (338) blank with imprint middle center; (339), (340) blanks; inserted following page (340) are 18 leaves of facsimile, being the facsimile of eight documents.

Blue paper boards, with tan cloth back strip, white paper spine label, upper front cover imprinted with the title in black upper center.

7 3/8 x 9 3/4

Privately printed. This volume, which, in itself, is of greatest interest, contains as the first and third facsimiles respectively at the end of the volume the first publication of "Magdalen" and "Harmodia." The paper is watermarked 'Van Gelder Zonen' and a script 'V G Z.' The edges have been evened, and many are untrimmed. Inserted inside the front cover is an 11-line slip concerning the distribution of the edition. There is no indication of the size of the edition.

POEMS ON HIS DOMESTIC CIRCUMSTANCES, &c &c   1816

London.   W. Hone.   Hay and Turner.

Contents: (1) title, (2) blank with imprint bottom center; (3) - 31 text of eight poems, (32) three-line note, with imprint bottom center. Issued with unsigned portrait of Byron facing title.

Thin brown drab wrappers, with elaborate title on outer front wrapper inside a printed border with imprint bottom center, and Hone advertisements on inside front wrapper and on both sides of the rear wrapper.

5 5/8 x 8 15/16

This is the sixth Hone edition of the largely spurious POEMS ON HIS DOMESTIC CIRCUMSTANCES, and carries the first publication of the ADIEU TO MALTA.

[*THE CURSE OF MINERVA*]

POEMS ON HIS DOMESTIC CIRCUMSTANCES, &c &c   *1816*

London.   W. Hone.   Hay and Turner

Contents: (1) title, (2) blank with imprint bottom center; (3) - 6 Memoir of Lord Byron, (7) - 32 text of nine poems. This pamphlet was issued with a portrait of Byron, unsigned, facing the title page.

Printed brown drab wrappers, with elaborate explanation and title on the front cover inside elaborate border with imprint bottom center, with Hone advertisements on inside front cover and on both sides of rear wrappers.

5 11/16 x 8 15/16

This is the eighth Hone edition. Pages 27-32 carry the first publication of THE CURSE OF MINERVA, which was privately printed in a small quarto edition in 1812. This is also the first Hone edition of POEMS ON HIS DOMESTIC CIRCUMSTANCES to carry the Memoir of Lord Byron, which is unsigned.

CONVERSATIONS OF LORD BYRON (by Thomas Medwin)

London.   Henry Coburn.   S. and R. Bentley

Contents: (i) half title, (ii) blank with imprint middle o (pages (iii) and (iv) are a folded facsimile of a lette Byron to J.C. Hobhouse); (v) title, (vi) blank; (vii) - x p (xi) - xxiii contents, (xxiv) blank; (1) - 351 text of th (352) blank; (i) fly title to the appendix, (ii) blank; (iii) - of 13 section appendix, with imprint at the bottom of p (civ) Coburn advertisements.

Drab brown boards with white paper spine label.

5 3/8 x 8 3/4

On pages 264-270 of this the new, or third, edition of CONVEF LORD BYRON appears the first publication of the complete pc AVATAR. This poem was written by Byron on September 1 copy sent to Thomas Moore in Paris, where Moore brought c printed edition of it the same year.

PART III

PRIVATELY PRINTED
AND SUPPRESSED EDITIONS
OF BYRON'S WORKS

Newark.   Printed by S. and J. Ridge.

Contents: (i) short title between double rules upper center, (ii) blank; (iii) dedication, (iv) nine-line note between double rules; (1) - 66 text of various poems, with imprint bottom center page 66.

Grey-green wrappers with no label.

7 1/2 x 8 3/4 (trimmed)

Byron's first book, privately printed, which was suppressed by Byron and only a handful of copies is known to have survived.

FUGITIVE PIECES (by I. Nathan)   1829

London.   Wittaker, Treacher, and Co.   Plummer and Brewis.

Contents: (i) half title, (ii) blank; (iii) title, (iv) imprint middle center; (v) - xviii preface; (xix) contents; (1) - 196 text with imprint lower center page 196; (1) - (12) (actually pages 197-208) advertisements for musical works.

Drab brown boards with green cloth spine with white paper spine label.

4 3/4 x 7 1/2

The first edition, which contains the first publication of three Byron poems, viz. 'I speak not - I trace not - I breathe not thy name' (page 64), 'In the valley of waters' (page 67) and 'They say that hope is happiness' (page 70).

According to the Elkins Matthews Catalogue (E.M., 30), "As long ago as 1884 NOTES AND QUERIES describes this book as 'not readily obtainable now' ". Scarce it remains.

London. Printed for Private Circulation. Chiswick Press.

Contents: (i) two-line note on the limitation of this edition, signed by 'Charles Whittingham & Co.' (ii) blank; (iii) half title, (iv) blank; (v) title, (vi) blank; (vii) - x 'Preface'; (xi) blank, (xii) blank; (1) - (70) facsimile of FUGITIVE PIECES, numbered (i) - (iv); (1) - 66 as in the original edition; (71) Chiswick Press imprint, (72) blank.

Very heavy, beveled edged boards covered with cream coloured imitation vellum, printed in gold on both covers and the spine.

8 3/4 x 10 15/16

This facsimile of FUGITIVE PIECES was printed in an edition of 100 copies for Harry Buxton Forman, from Forman's copy of the original, 1806, edition (The Becher-Faulkner-Ball-Forman-Wise Copy). Printed on very heavy paper watermarked 'W KING.'

New York. Facsimile Text Society. Columbia University Press.

Contents: (i) half title, (ii) blank; (iii) title, (iv) blank with imprint bottom center; (v) - (viii) bibliographical note; (1) - (70) reduced facsimile of FUGITIVE PIECES with original pagination preserved i.e. (i) - (iv); (1) - 66.

Brown cloth boards, spine printed in gold.

5 1/2 x 8

This is the eighth volume of the first series of the Facsimile Text Society.

Newark. Printed by S. and J. Ridge

Contents: (i) half title, (ii) blank; (iii) title, (iv) blank; (v) dedication, (vi) blank; (vii) note, (viii) blank; (ix) - 11 (sic) contents (pages (x) and (xi) are numbered 10 and 11), (xii) blank; (1) - 69 text of POEMS, (70) blank; (71) fly title to IMITATIONS AND TRANSLATIONS, (72) blank; (73) - 85 text of IMITATIONS AND TRANSLATIONS, (86) blank; (87) fly title to FUGITIVE PIECES, (88) blank; (89) - 144 text of FUGITIVE PIECES, with imprint bottom center page 144.

Green-grey boards with red paper spine label.

4 15/16 x 7 3/4

Byron's second volume of verse, privately printed in, according to Moore, an edition of 100 copies. In this copy, which belonged to Augusta Mary Byron, Byron's sister, pages 13, 14; 15, 16; 17, 18; 19, 20; 25, 26; 27, 28; 57, 58; and 141, 142 are cancel leaves.

ENGLISH BARDS AND SCOTCH REVIEWERS, FIFTH, SUPPRESSED EDITION.

The sheets of this fifth edition were printed in 1812 and issued with either a title page correctly numbered the fifth or with a title page numbered the fourth. As this edition was rigorously suppressed by John Murray II at any point where Cawthorn attempted to sell it, the fifth edition of ENGLISH BARDS AND SCOTCH REVIEWERS, with either title page, is an exceedingly great rarity.

ENGLISH BARDS AND SCOTCH REVIEWERS   *1816*

London.   Cawthorn.   Wilson.

Contents: (A half title with blank reverse, pages (i), (ii), was apparently never issued, though provided for in the pagination) (iii) title, (iv) blank; (v) - vii preface, (viii) blank; (1) - 83 text of the poem, (84) blank; (85) - 87 postscript, (88) Cawthorn advertisements with imprint bottom center page.

Brown drab paper boards with white paper spine label.

4 5/8 x 7 5/8

This the suppressed fifth edition was issued both with a title page numbered fifth edition and dated 1816 and with a title page numbered fourth edition and dated 1811. The title pages dated 1811 are part of the printing for the second fourth edition of 1811.

London.   Printed by T. Davison.

Contents: (1) title, (2) blank; (3) - 25 text of the poem, (26) blank; (27) blank with imprint middle center, (28) blank.

Dark brown glazed paper boards with no label.

8 13/16 x 11 3/16

The privately printed first issuance of this poem, which was first published in Philadelphia by de Silver & Co., 1815 (THE CURSE OF MINERVA). The first English publication was in the eighth edition of POEMS ON HIS DOMESTIC CIRCUMSTANCES, London, 1816 printed for W. Hone by Hay and Turner. Printed on paper with the watermark 'John Hall/1805,' or 'J Whatman/1810.'

THE WALTZ (By Horace Hornem, Esq.)   *1813, March*

London. Sherwood, Neely and Jones. S. Gosnell.

Contents: (1) title, (2) blank; (3) - (6) text of prose note 'To The Publisher'; (7) - 27 text of the poem, (28) blank. The imprint appears center bottom page 27.

Issued stabbed without wrapper.

8 7/8 x 11 1/16

The privately printed first issuance of this poem which was first published in Philadelphia in 1820 by Moses Thomas (THE WORKS OF THE RIGHT HONOURABLE LORD BYRON). This volume was the model for the first English publication, printed by and for W. Clark, London, 1821 (THE WALTZ).

The privately printed two variants of the first issue of THE GIAOUR should be included in this section, but for the sake of clarity and convenience, their descriptions have been given in PART I, in their chronological place.

London. (Probably Murray. Davison).

Contents: (1) - 3 text of poem with dropped head title page (1), (4) blank.

Issued unbound.

7 3/4 x 9 13/16

Privately printed in an edition of 50 copies, of which only a handful has survived.

The paper is watermarked 'J Green/1815.'

A SKETCH FROM PRIVATE LIFE   *1816, March 30*

London.   (Probably Murray.   Davison)

Contents: (1) - 4 text of the poem with a dropped head title top center page (1).

Issued unbound.

7 3/4 x 9 11/16

Privately printed in an edition of 50 copies, of which only a handful survives. The paper is watermarked 'J. Dickinson & Co/1811.'

Padua.   Printed in the Seminary of Padua.

Contents: (1) title page, (2) blank; (3) - 14 text of the poem and translations of it into 11 languages or dialects; (15) imprint center middle, (16) blank.

Issued stabbed without wrappers or label.

4 1/8 x 6 5/8

First edition, privately printed by the Hoppner family. On paper water-marked with a scroll and leaf. Only a handful of copies of this pamphlet survives and there is no reliable information on the size of the original edition.

Paris.

Contents: (1) short title middle center, (2) blank; (3) - 8 text of the poem.

Issued stabbed without wrappers or label.

5 1/2 x 8 11/16

The privately printed first appearance, of which 20 copies were printed in Paris at the order of Thomas Moore, to whom Byron had sent the poem in September 1821. Byron requested Moore to have these copies printed in his letter to Moore of September 20, 1821, and requested that six of the 20 copies be sent to the author in Pisa.

London.   John Pearson.

Contents: (1) half title, (2) note "One hundred copies privately
printed" upper middle; (3) title, (4) blank; (5) note, (6) blank;
(7) text of a Byron letter, (8) blank; (9) part of the text of the
poem, (10) blank; (11) the concluding portion of the poem, (12)
- (16) blanks.

Issued stitched without wrapper or label.

5 5/8 x 9

The first, privately printed, appearance in book form. This poem originally
appeared in the Morning Chronicle for March 2, 1812.

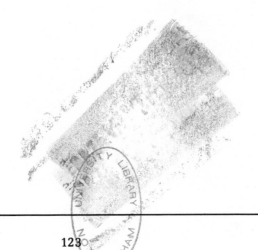